HACHETTE
GUIDE
TO
PARIS

PANTHEON BOOKS
NEW YORK

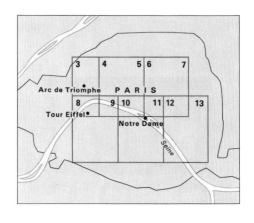

ISBN : 0-394-75436-0

ISSN : 0896-0151

Manufactured in the United States of America

First American Edition

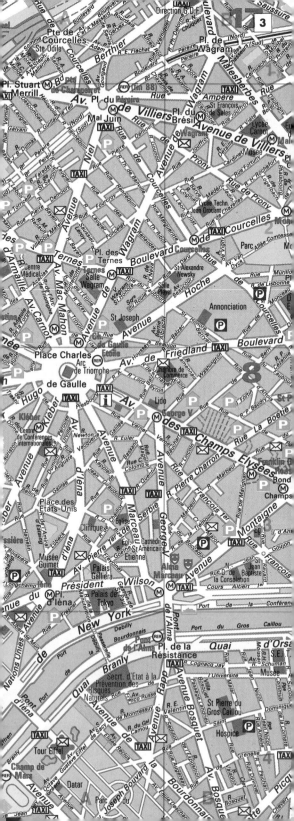

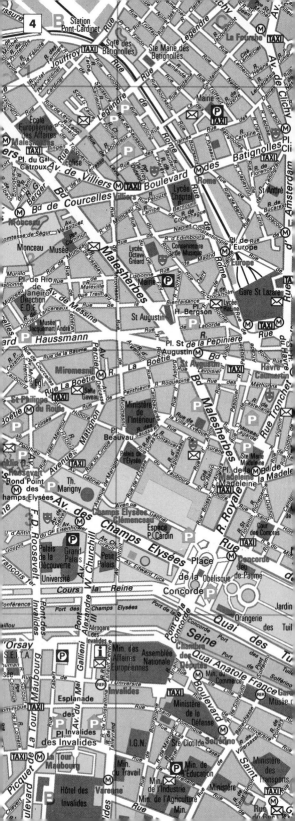

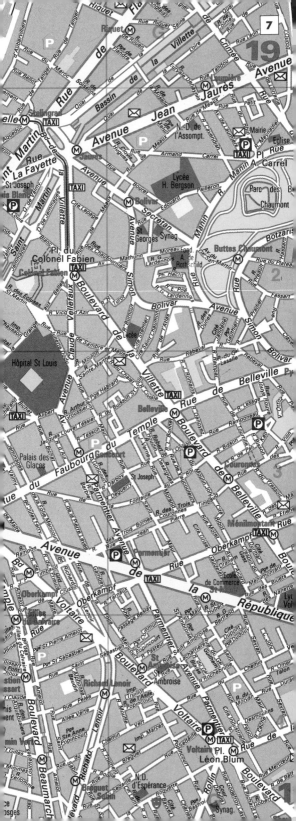

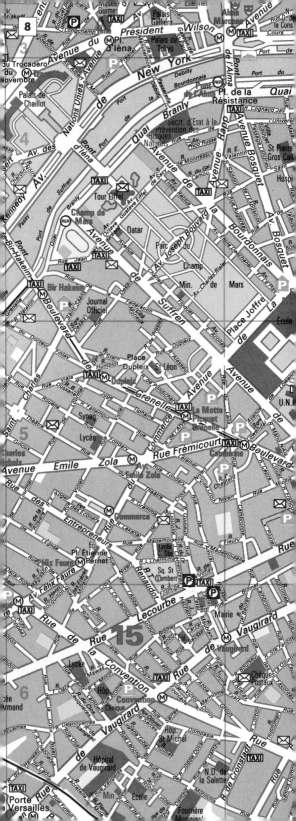

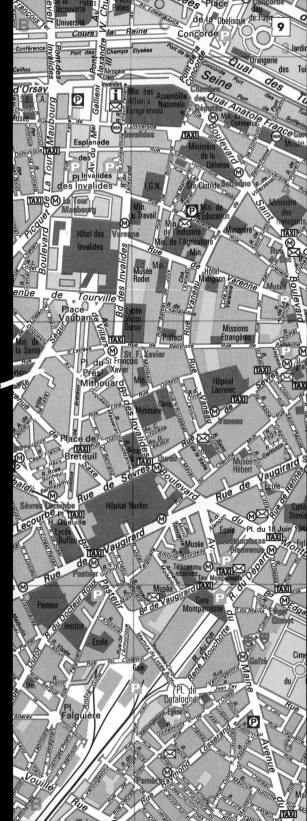

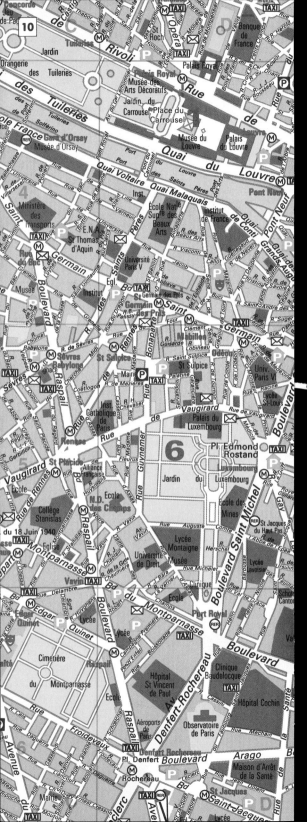

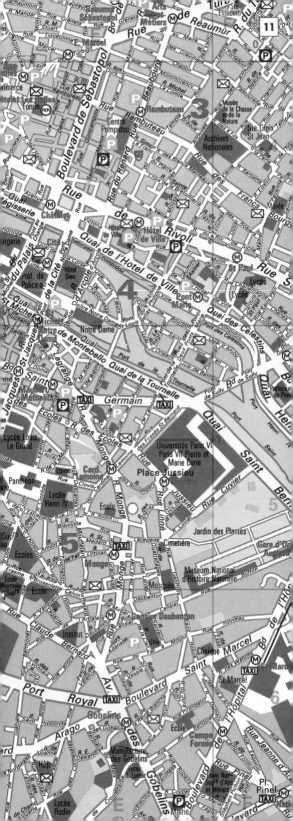

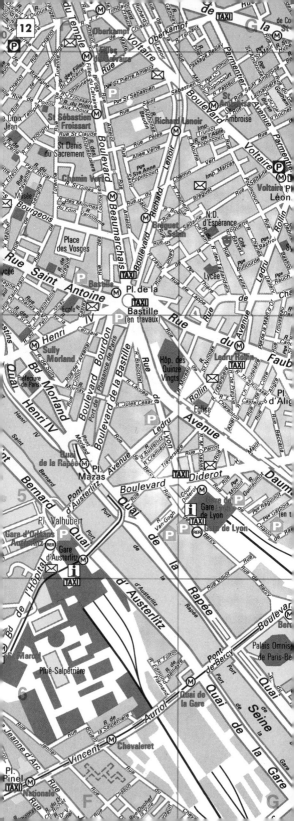

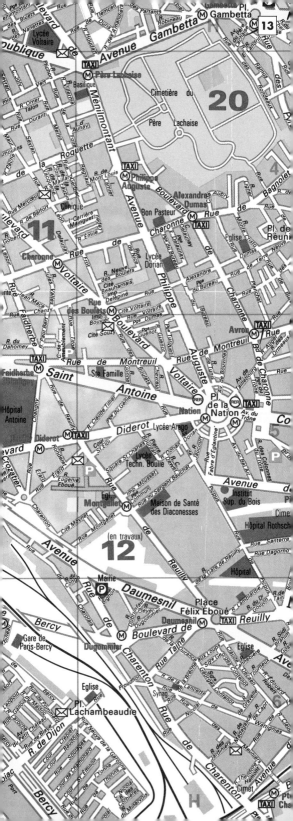

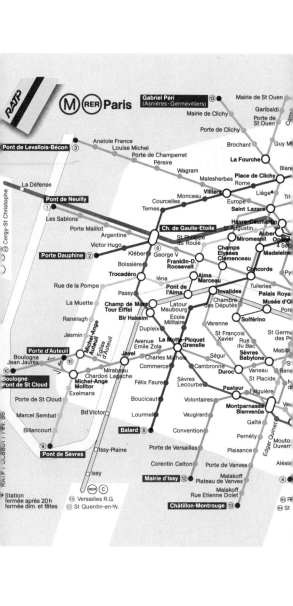

M RER Paris

Gabriel Péri ⑬
(Asnières-Gennevilliers)

Mairie de St Ouen
Garibaldi
Porte de
St Ouen

Mairie de Clichy

Porte de Clichy
Brochant   Guy M

Pont de Levallois-Bécon ③
Anatole France
Louise Michel
Porte de Champerret
Péreire
Wagram
Malesherbes

La Fourche
Blan

Place de Clichy

Rome
Liège⑬

La Défense
Villiers
Tri
Monceau
Europe
Courcelles   Saint Lazare
Ternes
Havre Caumartin
St Augustin
Miromesnil   Auber
Champs   4 Sep.
Elysées   Madeleine
Clémenceau

Cergy-St Christophe

Pont de Neuilly ①
Les Sablons
Porte Maillot
Argentine
Victor Hugo
Kléber
George V ⑥
St Philippe
du Roule
Ch. de Gaulle-Etoile

Porte Dauphine ②
Boissière
Franklin-D.
Roosevelt
Concorde   Py

Trocadéro
Iéna
Alma
Marceau
Tuileries
Palais Roya
Musée d'O

Rue de la Pompe
Passy
Pont de
l'Alma
Invalides
Chambre
des Députés
Solférino

La Muette
Champ de Mars
Tour Eiffel
Latour
Maubourg
Ecole
Militaire
St François
Xavier
St Germa
des Pe

Ranelagh
Bir Hakeim
Duplex
Varenne
Rue
du Bac
Mabillo

Jasmin
Michel-Ange
Auteuil
Eglise
d'Auteuil
Avenue
Emile Zola
La Motte-Picquet
Grenelle
Sèvres
Babylone
S

Porte d'Auteuil
Javel
Charles Michels
Ségur
Vaneau
Reni

Boulogne
Jean Jaurès
Commerce
Cambronne
Duroc
St Placide
N

⑩
Mirabeau
Chardon Lagache
Félix Faure
Sèvres
Lecourbe
Pasteur
Falguiè

Boulogne
Pont de St Cloud
Michel-Ange
Molitor
Exelmans
Boucicaut
Volontaires
Montparnasse
Bienvenüe
Vav

Porte de St Cloud
Bd Victor
Lourmel
Vaugirard
Gaîté

Marcel Sembat
Balard ⑧
Convention
Pernéty
Edgar Quinet

Billancourt
Issy-Plaine
Porte de Versailles
Plaisance
Mouto
Duver

⑨
Pont de Sèvres
Issy
Corentin Celton
Porte de Vanves
Alésia

RER Ⓒ
Versailles R.G.
St Quentin-en-Y.
Mairie d'Issy ⑫
Malakoff
Plateau de Vanves
④

Station
fermée après 20h
fermée dim. et fêtes
Malakoff
Rue Etienne Dolet
⑬ R
⑭ St

Châtillon-Montrouge ⑬

RATP P.C.8801 Fév. 88

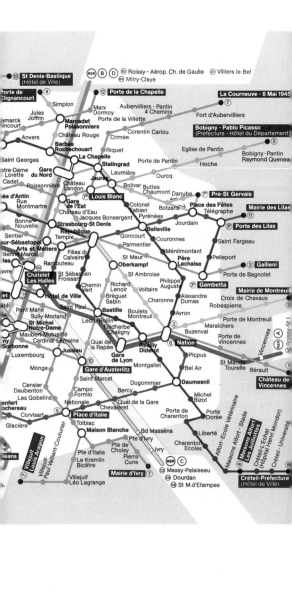

Map labels (Paris Métro map):

⑬ St Denis-Basilique
(Hôtel de Ville)

⑫ Porte de la Chapelle

⑦ Roissy – Aérop. Ch. de Gaulle   ⑰ Villiers le Bel
Ⓑ Ⓓ
Ⓚ Mitry-Claye

La Courneuve - 8 Mai 1945
⑦

Porte de
Clignancourt ④
Simplon
Marx
Dormay
Aubervilliers - Pantin
4 Chemins
Fort d'Aubervilliers

Jules
Joffrin
Lamarck
Caulaincourt
Marcadet
Poissonniers
Porte de la Villette

Corentin Cariou
Bobigny - Pablo Picasso
(Préfecture - Hôtel du Département)
⑤

Anvers
Château Rouge
Crimée
Eglise de Pantin
Bobigny - Pantin
Raymond Queneau

Saint Georges
Barbès
Rochechouart
La Chapelle
Riquet
Porte de Pantin
Hoche

Notre-Dame
de Lorette
Gare
du Nord
Stalingrad
Laumière
Ourcq

Cadet
Poissonnière
Château
Landon
Jaurès
Bolivar
Buttes
Chaumont
Danube
⑦ Pré-St Gervais

Chaussée d'Antin
Rue
Montmartre
Gare
de l'Est
Château d'Eau
Louis Blanc
Colonel
Fabien
Pyrénées
Botzaris
Place des Fêtes
Télégraphe
Mairie des Lilas

Bonne
Nouvelle
Strasbourg-St Denis
Jacques Bonsergent
Jourdain
⑦ Porte des Lilas

Sentier
Réaumur-Sébastopol
Étienne Marcel
République
Temple
Goncourt
Belleville
Couronnes
Saint Fargeau

Arts et Métiers
Filles du
Calvaire
Parmentier
Ménilmontant
Pelleport

Louvre
Rambuteau
St Sébastien
Froissart
St Maur
Oberkampf
Père
Lachaise
Gambetta
③ Gallieni

Châtelet
Les Halles
St Ambroise
Porte de Bagnolet

Hôtel de Ville
⑪
Chemin
Vert
Richard
Lenoir
Philippe
Auguste
Voltaire
Charonne
Mairie de Montreuil

Cité
Saint Paul
Bréguet
Sabin
Bastille
Boulets
Montreuil
Alexandre
Dumas
Croix de Chavaux
Robespierre

Pont Marie
Sully-Morland
St Michel
Notre-Dame
Ledru-Rollin
Faidherbe
Chaligny
Avron
Porte de Montreuil

Maubert-Mutualité
Cardinal Lemoine
Quai de
la Rapée
Reuilly
Diderot
②
Buzenval
Porte de
Vincennes

Sorbonne
Jussieu
Gare
de Lyon
Nation
Picpus
St Mandé
Tourelle
Vincennes Ⓐ
Bérault

Luxembourg
Monge
Saint Marcel
Montgallet
Bel Air
Château de
Vincennes
①

Censier
Daubenton
Gare d'Austerlitz
⑩
Dugommier
Daumesnil

Les Gobelins
Campo
Formio
Bercy
Michel
Bizot

Denfert
Rochereau
Nationale
Quai de la Gare
Porte
Dorée

Corvisart
Chevaleret
Porte de
Charenton

Glacière
Place d'Italie
Liberté
Maisons Alfort - Stade

Tolbiac
Bd Massena
Charenton
Ecoles
Maisons Alfort
Les Juilliottes

Villejuif
Louis Aragon
⑦
Maison Blanche
Pte d'Ivry
Ivry
Alfort-Ecole Vétérinaire
Créteil-L'Echat
(Hôpital Henri Mondor)

Villejuif
Paul Vaillant-Couturier
Pte d'Italie
Pte de
Choisy
Mairie d'Ivry
⑦
Massy-Palaiseau
Créteil-Université

Villejuif
Léo Lagrange
Le Kremlin
Bicêtre
Pierre
Curie
Ⓒ
Dourdan
St M.d'Etampes
Créteil-Préfecture
(Hôtel de Ville)
⑧

Paris

	Eisenbahn / Chemin de fer Railway / Ferrovia
◀◀◀	Einbahnstrasse / Rue à sens unique One-way street / Via a senso unico
	Fussgängerzone / Zone pour piétons Pedestrian area / Zone pedonale
	Öffentliches Gebäude / Bâtiment public Public building / Edificio pubblico
	Park, Sportplatz / Jardin, Terrain de sport Park, Sportsground / Parco, Campo sportivo
	Wald / Forêt Forest / Foresta
i **P**	Informationsbüro, Polizei / Syndicat d'Initiative, Police Tourist information center, Police / Ufficio informazione, Poliz
P	Parkhaus / Parking couvert Parking house / Garage pubblico
☻	Theater / Théâtre Theatre / Teatro
✉ **TAXI**	Post, Taxi / Bureau de poste, Taxi Post office, Taxi / Ufficio postale, Tassi
	Schiffsanlegestelle / Embarcadère Landing place / Debarcadero
Ⓜ Ⓡ	Station de métro, U-Bahn-Station, RER-Station / Station du RER Underground station. RER station / Stazione di metropolitana Stazione di RER
✈	Flughafen / Aéroport Airport / Aeroporto
♣ ♣	Schloss, Kirche / Château, Eglise Castle, Church / Castello, Chiesa
▲ L	Denkmal, Ruine / Monument, Ruine Monument, Ruin / Monumento, Rovina
▲	Campingplatz / Terrain de camping Camping site / Campeggio

Hallwag

Paris ●

▶ When you arrive in Paris, whether it is your first visit or your hundredth, there is always the same thrill of pleasure. The Seine; the lovely grey of Notre-Dame; the long walls of the Louvre; the sweep of the Tuileries, the Concorde and the Champs-Élysées; distant Montmartre; and the dizzying height of the Eiffel Tower. Then, in the evening, the lights and the surging crowds. You probably knew it was like this, even before you saw it: the Paris of the Impressionists — sung, painted and filmed exactly as it is.

But there is a hidden side to this wonderful city. The Parisians have a tendency to keep it to themselves — Paris belongs to them, after all. It's a living city, full of oddities, unexpected pleasures and (sometimes) disappointments; above all, a place with a deep sense of history, which rarely degenerates into nostalgia. This is the Paris we have sought to reveal in this guide.

The sheer amount of sights and experiences offered by this unique city may cause the first-time visitor to feel overwhelmed, and at a loss for a starting point. This is why we have included a number of articles dealing with practical subjects in this chapter, in addition to the regular practical information section at the end. Sites of interest are described in alphabetical order, but are also grouped by district, or *quartier,* in the chapter's opening pages. A full page is devoted to travel, with a list of bus routes that take the visitor through some of Paris' most interesting areas : a novel and authentically Parisian way to see the city. One-, three- and eight-day itineraries are also suggested : naturally these can be modified and adapted to the visitor's own tastes... □

Brief history

53 BC-AD 451

During the Gallic Wars, Caesar's army discovered a small township named **Lutetia** on what is now the Île de la Cité; it was inhabited by a small tribe called the **Parisii.** ● The Romans established themselves there, building a new town on the left bank of the river; with traffic thriving, the Seine boatmen's corporation acquired an importance that lasted for ten centuries. ● **Saint Denis,** bishop of the town, converted the Parisii to Christianity, but was beheaded on the Butte Montmartre in the year 250. Two centuries later, **Saint Geneviève,** a shepherdess from Nanterre, rallied the Parisians in their successful resistance to Attila's invading Huns (451).

5th-10thC

Clovis was the first Christian chieftain of the whole of Gaul; he chose Paris as his capital and died there in 511. His successors extended and beautified the city. **King Dagobert** was buried at Saint-Denis. ● **Charlemagne** preferred Rome and Aix-la-Chapelle to Paris — his descendents signally failed to defend the city against the Norman onslaught. Paris was once more reduced to a small island town during the siege of 885-886.

10th-15thC

With the arrival of the Capetian kings on the throne of France, Paris once more became a centre of political power. Its mercantile prosperity favoured the Seine's right bank, which was low-lying and marshy; **Les Halles** (central markets) were founded in 1137, and remained on the same site for more than eight hundred years. ● The churches and royal palace of the Île de la Cité were joined in the 12thC by the **Cathedral of Notre-Dame,** which was begun in 1163. The City's subsequent development obliged **King Philip Augustus** to build a defensive rampart, culminating in the fortress of the **Louvre** (1190). ● The left bank once more entered the picture with the foundation of the **University.** Meanwhile, the reputation of Paris was spreading. Saint Louis and Philippe le Bel built the **Sainte Chapelle** and extended the royal palace on the Île de la Cité. The population soon surpassed 200 000, and Paris became a focus for political, religious, economic and intellectual power. ● The revolt led by the ambitious merchant-provost Étienne Marcel created a deep and lasting suspicion of the subversive Paris populace in the minds of the French monarchs. Subsequently, the city was brought to the brink of ruin by the **Hundred Years' War.**

16th-18thC

Louis XII established the first grand rules for urban development; François I then tackled the reconstruction of the Louvre Palace, widened streets and forced the municipality to build a **Hôtel de Ville** (town hall) worthy of Paris. His reign marked the beginning of a veritable renaissance, during which the city acquired immense **intellectual prestige.** The Wars of Religion broke out in 1572, and eventually led to the devastation of part of the city. Henri IV quickly rebuilt it after his conversion to Catholicism, leaving, with the able assistance of Sully, a lasting testimonial to his concern for urban planning. Private promoters followed the King's example, and new *quartiers* sprang up all around (Île St. Louis, Faubourg Montmartre, Faubourg St. Germain, Faubourg St. Honoré, with the various mansions built by Mansart) along with religious foundations (Val-de-Grâce) spearheading the reaction against Protestantism. ● Louis XIV cared little for Paris after the **Fronde insurrections**; despite the triumphal arches he erected in the city (Porte St. Denis and Porte St. Martin) and the Paris squares built around his statue (Place des Victoires, Place Vendôme), the Sun King preferred his palace of Versailles. ● The 18thC was a period of unprecedented **economic growth.** For the first time, private houses were built with an eye to real comfort : Louis XV set about a number of major building projects within Paris (Place de la Concorde, Panthéon, Saint-Sulpice, École Militaire). On the eve of the Revolution, the population of Paris had increased to around 650 000. ● The Revolution left no buildings of note. On the contrary, its influence was mainly destructive ; after the Bastille, many convents, churches and aristocratic mansions were pulled down. More seriously in terms of the future, the parks belonging to the nobility and the religious orders were annexed for other purposes — thus Paris was deprived of all its green spaces.

19thC

Napoléon turned Paris into the **capital** of his empire. His **organizational genius** was applied to the city's roads, drains and water supply, as well as to major public building projects like the Arc de Triomphe at the Carrousel, the Arc de Triomphe at the Étoile, the Stock Exchange (Bourse) and the Madeleine. ● Napoléon's ambitious street-widening projects were not realized till the arrival of **Haussmann** during the **Second Empire.** Meanwhile, apartment blocks and buildings swelled the faubourgs of Paris northward and eastward ; these became hotbeds of revolution in 1830 and 1848. ● Napoléon III collected a remarkable team of planners to **reorganize Paris.** In the space of 15 years, he created a modern city. Broad boulevards pierced the tangled alleys of former ages (Saint-Michel, de Sébastopol, de Strasbourg, de Magenta, Voltaire, Diderot, Saint-Germain, Malesherbes and Haussmann). The Baron Haussmann made it possible to get around Paris ; and Alphand, with his green parks and gardens, made it possible to breathe (Parc Monceau, Buttes-Chaumont, Bois de Vincennes and Bois de Boulogne). At this period, the city swallowed up its faubourgs and inner suburbs, Auteuil, Passy, La Chapelle, Belleville, Bercy, Grenelle and Vaugirard. ● The **Commune,** a socialist/anarchist insurrection among the Paris populace, was bloodily repressed in May 1871 following Napoléon III's defeat by the Prussians at Sedan. The advent of the Third Republic saw a resumption of the capital's expansion. The Basilica of Sacré-Cœur (Montmartre) was built at this time, with construction in steel enjoying an immense vogue. The **Eiffel Tower,** steel's unrivaled showpiece, appeared in 1889. Development was also underway beneath the surface ; drains, water pipes and electricity cables were laid. The first **Metropolitan Railway** (Métro) line opened in 1900.

20thC

The turn of the century, the **Belle Époque** to which a few Métro stations and buildings still bear witness, was quickly submerged in the 1914-1918 War. Paris emerged from this holocaust, only to plunge immediately into profound political and economic crisis. Concrete was used for the first time as a building material (Champs-Élysées Theatre) whilst the first low-rent apartment buildings significantly failed to relieve an acute **housing shortage.** ● During the **German Occupation** (June 1940-August 1944), a time of strict rationing, fear and Gestapo raids was offset by glittering and provocative night-life and real intellectual and artistic creativity. After the resistance uprising of the 19th and 20th August 1944, General Philippe Leclerc's tank division at last entered Paris on the 24th. ● Once it had been liberated by Allied forces, Paris undertook an intense effort of **reconstruction** and **modernization.** The 1950's witnessed a crop of somewhat featureless buildings, and it was only in the 1960s that the "International" architectural style (glass, steel and aluminium) made its first appearance. (U.N.E.S.C.O. building, Maison de la Radio, Maine-Montparnasse complex, Palais des Congrès). ● Traffic and supply problems led to the demolition of the iron-structured Halles de Baltard (Central Market) in 1970, and to the controversial opening of the Seine bank expressways (Voies Express). ● In 1977, for the first time in history, Paris elected a **mayor.**

Unusual museums :
Musée du vin

The Wine Museum, situated in a former quarry under the ground, offers an initiation into the art of cultivating vines and the techniques of vinification (Rue des Eaux, 16th arr., 10-6 daily).

● *Around Paris*

▶ **ALBERT KAHN Gardens***

9, Quai du 4-Septembre, Boulogne-Billancourt. Métro : Pont-de-Saint-Cloud. Bus : 52, 72.

The Albert Kahn Gardens (Jardins Albert-Kahn) are as filled with contrasts as the life of the turn-of-the-century adventurer for whom they are named. Extraordinary juxtaposition of pinewoods, rock garden, orchard, English park, Japanese garden; astonishingly varied collection of flowers from all over the world. A veritable garden museum *(9:30-12:30 & 2-6 ; 15 Mar.-15 Nov.).* □

▶ ARC DE TRIOMPHE**

Map 3-A4 / Place Charles-de-Gaulle. 8th, 16th, 17th arr.
Métro and RER : Étoile-Charles-de-Gaulle. Bus : 22, 30,
31, 43, 52, 73, 83, 92. Access to the monument via underground passage at top of Ave. des Champs-Élysées.

For over 150 years, the Arc de Triomphe in what is
now the Place Charles-de-Gaulle has been a symbol of French patriotism; it also commemorates the
heroes and the fallen of past wars. The colossal arch,
built on the raised site of the former "Étoile de Chaillot" (Star of Chaillot) is the hub upon which twelve
broad avenues converge like the spokes of a wheel. A
project for a national monument was adopted during
the Revolution, but construction did not start until
1806 when Napoléon approved Chalgrin's design for
a triumphal arch "... except" (in his words), "for the
embellishments, which are bad." The fall of the Empire
put work on the Arc into abeyance for so long that it
became a standing joke for Parisians. Finally, Louis-
Philippe inaugurated it, still unfinished, in 1836. The
original plans called for the erection of a huge star or
quadriga on the top of the building — an idea which
has now been abandoned forever.

▶ Nonetheless, the Arc de Triomphe, as it stands, is most
impressive. Its massive proportions (50 m high by 40 m
wide) combine with the vigour of its decorative reliefs
to produce an effect of great power. The best-known
of these reliefs is Rude's "La Marseillaise"★ (on the right,
from the Champs-Élysées). An idea of the sheer scale of
the building is given by the frieze of figures around its
top, all of which are larger than life. The Arc may be unfinished, but it amply fulfills its role as a national symbol
commemorating the glories of the Empire along with
France's "Unknown Soldier", for whom a flame is kept
constantly alight within the building by war veterans. Visitors, however, will probably prefer the view from the Arc's
summit (10-5) to the wreaths, the flags and the ceremonies of Bastille Day (14th of July). **Panorama★** of the
whole city, from the towers of La Défense to Montmartre
and the Panthéon.   □

Unusual museums :
Monocle Museum

*Dalaï-lama's eyeglasses are displayed right
next to Sarah Bernhardt's, along with a fantastic
collection of monocles, pince-nez, opera-glasses, etc.
This collection by optician Pierre Marly is worth a look !
(Musée des Lunettes et Lorgnettes de jadis, Pierre
Marly, 2, Av. Mozart, 16th arr., tel. : 45.27.21.05,
9 :30-12 & 2-6 :30, closed Sun.).*

▶ Musée d'ART MODERNE DE LA
VILLE DE PARIS**
(Museum of Modern Art)

Map 8-A4 / 11, Avenue du Président-Wilson, 16th arr.
Métro : Iéna, Alma-Marceau. RER : Pont de l'Alma. Bus :
32, 42, 63, 72, 80, 82, 92.

This museum has been completely refurbished since
the National Museum's collections were moved to the
Pompidou Centre, better adapted for exhibitions of
contemporary art. The Museum of Modern Art now
displays important cubist, fauvist and Paris school
paintings. Furthermore, the Centre National de la Pho-
tographie organizes many shows here.

▶ Matisse's famous triptych, La Danse★ is here,
alongside Dufy's gigantic Fée Electricité★, one of the larg-

est murals ever painted. ▶ There is still a whiff of scandal and provocation about the Museum of Modern Art : the ARC section (Animation-Research-Confrontation) organizes demonstrations of contemporary art which are receptive to all the trends of the avant-garde. The plastic arts rub shoulders here with jazz and poetry ; the result is sometimes "over-contemporary" — but always exciting *(10-5:30 or 8 Wed. ; closed Mon.).* ☐

▶ Musée des ARTS DÉCORATIFS* and Musée national des ARTS DE LA MODE*

(Museum of Decorative Arts and Museum of the Arts of Fashion)

Map 10-D5 / 107-109, Rue de Rivoli, 1st arr. Métro : Palais-Royal, Tuileries. Bus : 21, 27, 39, 48, 68, 69, 72, 85.

The Museum of Decorative Arts was opened in 1905 in the Marsan Pavilion, rebuilt after the fire that destroyed the Tuileries Palace in 1871.

▶ Reopened in 1985, the museum exhibits some 80,000 pieces, including furniture, decorative objects, jewelry, *boiseries* (woodwork, especially paneling) and tapestries, from the 15thC to the present day. Other European countries are also represented, along with the art of Islam. A contemporary gallery reuniting for the first time the collections of the 20thC and the Dubuffet gallery. Three documentary rooms : glass, textiles and wallpaper. Art studios open to adults and children *(12:30-6:30 ex Mon. and Tue. ; 11-5 Sun.).*

▶ Opened at the end of 1985, the Museum of Fashion presents the evolution of the arts of dress over an area of 2000 m². Alongside the permanent collections one can trace the contemporary development of fashion day by day *(same hours as above).* ☐

▶ Musée des ARTS ET TRADITIONS POPULAIRES**

(Museum of Popular Arts and Traditions)

Map p. 58-59 A1, 59 / 6, route du Mahatma-Gandhi, 16th arr. (Bois de Boulogne). Métro : Porte-Maillot, Sablons. Bus : 73 ; 33 Sat. and Sun.

The aim of this highly individual museum is to breathe new life into the traditions of rural France, to display the wealth and variety of the nation's crafts, and to demonstrate the beauty and value of the tools and skills of an earlier time. The collection touches on every aspect of rural life ; the games, entertainments and dances of provincial France all have their place here, along with traditional tools, utensils, crockery, pottery and a wide range of farm implements *(10-5:15 ex Tue.).* ☐

▶ Place de la BASTILLE

Map 12-F5 / 4th, 11th, 12th arr. Métro : Bastille. Bus : 29, 65, 69, 76, 86, 87, 91.

The Bastille is a lively, popular *quartier* which used to be a centre for nocturnal revelry among the Paris riffraff. The dance-halls in the Rue de Lappe used to be especially popular with the local *apaches* and *marlous* (hooligans). Today the "Balajo" dance-hall still keeps alive the tradition of the *java* and *bal musette* (accordeon balls).

▶ The **Faubourg St. Antoine** is now almost entirely given over to the sale of reproduction period furniture, but during the last century it seethed with workers and artisans who played an important part in the social upheavals and riots of 1830 and 1848. ▶ The Bastille is the rallying point for workers' unions, which hold their demonstrations around the **Colonne de Juillet** (July Column)★ crowned with its Spirit of Liberty. ▶ The Colonne de Juillet is all that remains of the eight-towered fortress destroyed in the Revolution. ▶ The 1989 opening of the **Opéra de la Bastille** will contribute to the rejuvenation of this popular neighborhood.   □

Paris-on-the-Seine

On the Canal St-Martin, at the foot of the Bastille column, the dream has become reality : Paris has a port, le port de l'Arsenal. This pleasure-boat marina's amenities include an ultra-modern harbour-master office, a shop selling boating equipment, a restaurant and flowered promenades. A lovely starting-point for river cruisers who wish to explore the Marne, the Seine and even the open sea.

▶ BOIS DE BOULOGNE*

Map p. 58-59 A2 / 16th arr. between Neuilly and Boulogne. Métro : Porte-Maillot, Porte-Dauphine, Porte d'Auteuil, Sablons. Bus : PC, 32, 52, 63 ; 33 Sat. and Sun.

▶ The Bois was ruthlessly cut down during the Revolution and again by the occupying British Army in 1815. Subsequently, it was rearranged according to Second Empire tastes as a park enlivened by **lakes, racecourses** (Auteuil and Longchamp) and a miniature railway track. On fine days, you can go boating on the lakes, which were designed by the engineer Alphand as part of a complicated network of watercourses fed by an artesian well. ▶ The miniature railway still carries children around the **Jardin d'Acclimatation** *(Sablons crossroads ; 9-dusk),* so called because various exotic creatures are acclimatized here to Paris temperatures : but children seem to prefer the goats, chickens and sheep of the "Farm" to the resident monkeys and parrots. The Jardin also has an extremely well-equipped and varied children's fun fair. ▶ "Papa Meilland", "Princess Ann" and "Sissi" are the stars of the **Bagatelle Park**★★ *(Porte-de-Madrid crossroads) ;* all three are species of rose. The rose gardens here are the most popular part of this much-loved park, landscaped around a splendid folly. The latter was built by the Count of Artois, who had a bet with the Queen of France that he could finish the job inside two months. The Count requisitioned all the stone and plaster available in Paris and had 900 labourers working round the clock ; the Queen lost her wager. ▶ In the humid **Municipal Greenhouses** (Serres du Fleuriste Municipal, av. de la Porte d'Auteuil, 10-5 or 6), it's hard to believe that you are only a few metres above the roaring *Boulevard Périphérique* (ring road) and alongside the gigantic **Parc des Princes**. Well-planned and cared for, this garden has a splendid orchid collection and a romantic **jardin des poètes**. ▶ The Bois has sporting facilities (tennis courts at Roland-Garros, clay-pigeon shooting) along with a large number of restaurants.   □

▶ BUTTES-CHAUMONT

Map 7-G3 / 19th arr. Métro : Buttes-Chaumont. Bus : 26, 60, 75.

With its sixty acres of rolling parkland, green enough to make a mockery of its name (*monts chauves* — literally, bald hills), the Buttes-Chaumont is perhaps Paris' most picturesque and surprising park, a kind of fantasy garden of the 18th century.

▶ The Buttes-Chaumont Park straddles the twin quartiers of **Belleville** and **Ménilmontant,** which at one time were typically Parisian. After the war, they were taken over by a large North African population which was in turn forced out in recent years by massive construction projects. Édith Piaf and Maurice Chevalier would never recognize their beloved "Ménilmuche" these days, unless they happened upon the hard-to-find entrance to the protected gardens near the Rues des Cascades or Bidassoa. □

▶ CARNAVALET Museum**

Map 12-F5 / 23, Rue de Sévigné, 3rd arr. Métro : Saint-Paul, Chemin-Vert. Bus : 29, 69, 76, 96.

Four centuries of Paris life (1500-1900) are vividly displayed in this splendid Renaissance mansion, redesigned by Mansart in the 17thC and decorated with large reliefs★ by Jean Goujon, and now a fit setting for the collections of the **Historical Museum of the City of Paris.** As an introduction to the history of Paris, this museum and its new annex in the **Hôtel Le Peletier de Saint-Fargeau** have no equal.

▶ Once the residence of Madame de Sévigné, the Carnavalet Museum has been conceived as a showpiece *(10-5:40; closed Mon.)* : fine furniture (Regency, Louis XV and Louis XVI, *boiseries,* gilt cabinet★★ painted by Le Brun), also period paintings, street scenes, shop signs, maps, and even an accurately-reconstructed café. □

▶ The CATACOMBS

Map 10-D7 / Place Denfert-Rochereau, 14th arr. Métro and RER : Denfert-Rochereau. Bus : 38, 68.

A veritable City of Death, the Catacombs can be entered through the E pavilion on the Place Denfert-Rochereau, a vestige of the old Barrière d'Enfer (Hell's Gate) in the city walls erected in 1784. They are really gigantic stone quarries used from 1785 as a dump for corpses from the cemetery of Les Innocents, near Les Halles, which had become so crowded that it was a constant danger to public health.

▶ The mortal remains of some thirty generations of Parisians were deposited in the Catacombs ; some of the bones and skulls were laid out in geometrical patterns by anonymous agents with a taste for the macabre *(2-4, closed Mon. ; 9-11 & 2-4 Sat.).* □

▶ CENTRE GEORGES-POMPIDOU**
(Beaubourg)

Map 11-E5 / Rue Saint-Martin, 4th arr. Métro : Châtelet, Les Halles, Hôtel-de-Ville, Rambuteau. RER : Châtelet-Les Halles. Bus : 38, 47, 58, 67, 69, 70, 72, 74, 85, 96.

The Centre National d'Art et de Culture Georges-Pompidou, better known as the Beaubourg or Pompidou Centre, was created at the behest of a former French President, Georges Pompidou (1969-1978). The aim of the Centre was to bring together in one place all the various trends in contemporary art forms with a view to acquainting the public at large with modern art and bringing creativity into the museum. This project, spurred on by France's rapid growth and prosperity during the early 1970s, has fulfilled its promise beyond all expectations *(12-10 pm daily; 10-10, Sat. and Sun. ; closed Tue., call (1) 42.77.11.12 for recorded information).*

▶ On the ground floor **piazza** level, the **forum** is dominated by a portrait of Georges Pompidou by Vasarely. Nearby are the reception and bookshop, next to the **salles d'actualité** (news rooms) of the Centre's library (reviews and recent publications), the CCI (Industrial Creation Centre) and **children's workshops.** On the mezzanine (street level), the CCI organizes original exhibitions which are a must for anyone interested in contemporary topics such as comic-strip art, the media, urban architecture. ▶ On the first, second and third floors, the **Public Information Library** (Bibliothèque Publique d'Information, BPI) displays books and periodicals and operates audio-visual equipment and cassettes in ninety-five foreign languages. The BPI's total surface area, all of which is freely accessible, amounts to something like four acres of floor space. ▶ Part of the third floor, and the whole of the fourth floor is devoted to the works of artists born after 1865. This is the **National Museum of Modern Art★★★**, recently reorganized, which exhibits all the great names of the 20thC : Bonnard, Picasso, Pollock, Mathieu, etc. Works by Kandinsky, along with Matisse's bronzes, and paintings by Max Ernst, the sculptures of Gonzalez and Miró, dominate a slightly uneven collection, which nonetheless demonstrates the fundamentally hesitant, questing nature of contemporary art. ▶ The fifth floor, which is the top, is the home of the **Cinémathèque** (film library and archives), along with certain temporary exhibitions, a bar and a restaurant. The **view★★** from here (40 m above ground level) is superb — the rooftops of all central Paris. ▶ All around the Pompidou Centre, the Piazza (once the **Plateau Beaubourg**) is now a pedestrian precinct. Bookshops, galleries and restaurants have replaced the former sordid haunts of the **Quartier de l'Horloge** (the Clock Quarter). The latter has become a modern building complex, almost a pastiche of the many styles that lurk behind the venerable facades of the **Rue St-Martin** ; fittingly, somehow, a clockwork armed man emerges to do battle with a monster, at the stroke of every hour — over the shop of J. Monestier, Rue Bernard-de-Clairvaux. On the other side, toward the Saint-Merri church, see the lively fountain★ designed by Jean Tinguely and Niki de Saint-Phalle (1983), above Pierre Boulez' IRCAM (Contemporary Musical and Acoustical Research Institute).   □

Unusual museums :
Musée d'Ennery

The Musée d'Ennery is an "atmospheric" museum, one among many others in Paris. The difference here is that the atmosphere is a very strong one, since the collections are entirely devoted to Far Eastern art, and plenty of it : the rooms are so crammed with statues and objects that their quality is almost submerged. The best items are doubtless the netsukés and kogos, skilfully worked buttons and boxes illustrating everyday scenes in the 17th and 18thC. The sense of detail and decorative precision shown in these objects makes each one a work of art in itself, and gives the Musée d'Ennery its particular distinction as a museum of miniature art (59 Ave. Foch, 16th arr., Thu. and Sun., 2-5 only).

▶ Palais de CHAILLOT*

Map 8-A5 / 16th arr. Métro : Trocadéro. Bus : 22, 30, 32, 63, 72, 82.

Seen from the Seine, the steep bank of Chaillot has a strangely theatrical air, almost grandiose. The site caught the fancy of Napoléon III, who leveled its summit. The organizers of the Great Exhibition of 1878 were inspired to build a Moorish Palace here ; their successors of 1937 constructed the present enormous building, the Palais de Chaillot, with two wings 200 m long, curving outward toward the Seine.

▶ The **Palais de Chaillot** is a prime example of the sober, somewhat cold architectural outlook of the 1930s. It now houses a huge **theatre,** made famous by Jean Vilar and the Théâtre National de Paris ; a **Cinémathèque** (film

library and archives), created by Henri Langlois (entrance Ave. A.-de-Mun); the **Naval Museum★★** (history of navigation : nautical instruments, *10-6; closed Tue. and hols.*); the **Musée de l'Homme★★** (Museum of Anthropology — human evolution and man's origins, *9:45-5:15; closed Tue.*); and the **Museum of French Monuments★★** (anthology of French sculpture, *9:45-12:30 & 2-5; closed Tue.*). All entrances are marked on the **Place du Trocadéro**.
▶ Below the Palais, in a cave built under the sloping gardens, is the **Aquarium★**; freshwater fish in somewhat hallucinatory surroundings (*10-6 daily*). The terraces of the Place du Trocadéro offer one of the loveliest views of the left Bank : the Eiffel Tower straddling the Champ-de-Mars gardens and École Militaire, the distant Montparnasse skyscraper and, to the right, the modern tower blocks of the Front de Seine.   □

▶ CHAMP-DE-MARS*

Map 8-A5 / 7th arr. Métro : École-Militaire, Bir-Hakeim; RER : Champ-de-Mars. Bus : 28, 42, 49, 69, 80, 82, 87, 92.

The Champ-de-Mars used to be a training ground for military manœuvres, where the soldiers from the **École Militaire★★** (Military Academy; architect : Gabriel; completed 1773) were put through their paces before the king. Here the young Napoléon Bonaparte studied the art of war. The Revolution evicted the army and used the Champ-de-Mars for its own ceremonial purposes, such as the Fête de la Fédération on 14 July 1790, at which the king and no less than 300 000 people from all over France swore fidelity to the nation before General Lafayette. Parades, festivals and horseraces took place here before the great universal exhibitions of 1867 and 1889. The Eiffel Tower, which provoked the furious indignation of the local inhabitants while it was under construction, has since been a magnet for tourists.   □

Shopping in Paris

Most visitors to Paris see it as the capital of French luxury commerce, fashion and the art of good living. Yet Paris owes a lot to talented foreigners living here, who have become some of its greatest creators : Japanese and Italians for fashion and luxury goods, Greeks for jewelry, even Englishmen for wines! As to fashion, you will always find in Paris the great names of the past, the severe, the outrageous, the avant-garde, haute-couture and ready-to-wear, along with the traditional fashion strongholds like the Faubourg St. Honoré, Place des Victoires, Boulevard des Capucines, St-Germain-des-Prés and Les Halles. One piece of advice : if you want to save time, go straight to see "what people are wearing" in the two leading department stores, Printemps and Galeries Lafayette. See also the list of good shopping addresses in the following pages.

▶ CHAMPS-ÉLYSÉES***

Map 3-B4 / 8th arr. Métro : Étoile, George-V, Champs-Élysées-Clemenceau, Concorde. RER : Étoile. Bus : 28, 30, 31, 42, 49, 52, 73, 80, 83, 92.

The Champs-Élysées avenue spans 2 km, from the Imperial and Republican Arc de Triomphe to the Royalist Tuileries gardens. Far off to the west can be seen the modern towers of Porte Maillot and La Défense.

▶ Before Le Nôtre planted his avenue of elms, there was nothing here but scrubland and marshes. Once lengthened and widened, the old Grand Cours became a meeting place for revolutionaries and ruffians, before developing into a site for theatres, puppet shows and gaming houses. In 1800, there were only six buildings on the Avenue; nor did it acquire its present aspect till a hundred years later. Office blocks, stores and cafés stretch from the Rond-Point to the Étoile, whilst among the trees between the Rond-Point and the Tuileries stand a number of theatres and restaurants. ▶ There are few monuments of note in this area, apart perhaps from the gaudy mansion of La Païva★ at No. 25, where the well-known courtesan used to give her famous parties... and the "Lido", a monument of Paris nightlife which has serenely weathered both the vicissitudes of history and the challenge of the daring and modern "Crazy Horse" nearby. The present world-wide fame of the Champ-Élysées is largely due to the superb setting it provides as the centre of Paris-by-night.   □

▶ CHÂTELET

Map 11-E5 / 1st arr. Métro and RER : Châtelet. Bus : 21, 24, 27, 38, 47, 58, 67, 69, 70, 72, 74, 75, 76, 81, 85, 96.

Around a 19thC fountain ("return from Egypt"), the **Place du Châtelet** marks the convergence of the main north-south and east-west traffic through the capital, both on the surface and underground (two RER lines cross here).

▶ On the Square, the **Théâtre de la Ville** (Municipal Theatre) has been successfully modernized — though it retains the dressing room of the great tragic actress Sarah Bernhardt in its original condition, as a kind of intimate museum. The theatre itself was constructed by Davioud in 1862, like the **Théâtre Musical de Paris** (TMP) opposite. The latter used to be known as the Châtelet Theatre, and was renowned for its operetta productions; now ballet and opera have returned here. ▶ Close by is the **St. Jacques Tower★**, beloved of the Surrealists, which adds a touch of the unusual to this quartier as it submits to the daily nightmarish traffic jams. It was completed in 1522 as the bell tower of the old church of St. Jacques-de-la-Boucherie, headquarters of a once-powerful corporation of butchers. The Revolution would have swept away the entire structure, had it not been for a gunsmith who used it as a shot-tower for making musket balls.   □

▶ Île de la CITÉ*

Map 11-E5-6 / 1st and 4th arr. Métro : Cité. Bus : 21, 24, 27, 38, 47, 58, 70, 85, 96.

The Île de la Cité, often compared to a boat's hull carried by the Seine, is the original core from which Paris developed. Its inhabitants have to some extent departed; the great mass of the Palais de Justice now overshadows the island's few remaining Louis XIII houses, and its medieval buildings were long ago torn down by Haussmann. Nonetheless, the Île de la Cité remains the living heart of Paris. Here, 20 centuries ago, one of Julius Caesar's lieutenants first set up his headquarters close to a village inhabited by the Parisii...

▶ The **Pont Neuf★** spans the Seine and takes in the western (downstream) end of the Île de la Cité. This bridge is ill-named, because, far from being "Neuf" (new), it is the oldest bridge Paris can boast. It is also the best-loved, most painted and most praised by poets. ▶ The statue of Henri IV, who inaugurated the Pont Neuf in 1607, dominates what is today the **Square du Vert-Galant**, a delightfully cool little garden on the tip of the island, much frequented on hot summer nights. ▶ The quiet **Place Dauphine★**, between two elegant Louis XIII buildings in brick and stone, was created in honour of the Dauphin. ▶ Enlarged under the Second Empire and at the turn of the century, the **Palais de Justice** (Law Courts)★ retains a considerable proportion of the original Gothic palace inhabited by the first twelve Capetian kings of France. Steer clear of the somewhat forbidding walls of the Quai des Orfèvres : more interesting is the **Quai de l'Horloge★**, to the N of the Palais. On this side, the façade is flanked by three round towers ; on the left, the entrance to the **Conciergerie★★,** an imposing edifice which owes much of its medieval haughtiness to 19thC restoration *(10-5 daily)*. Visit here the Prisoner's Gallery (cells occupied by Marie-Antoinette and Robespierre) and a small museum of the Revolution which occupies the chapel. The most remarkable aspect of this gaol-cum-palace, so laden with tragic memories, is the huge **Salle des Gens d'Armes★★**, with its four naves (1315). ▶ At the corner of the Quai de l'Horloge and the Boulevard du Palais stands the massive square tower known as the "Tour de l'Horloge" (Clocktower). This has kept time for the people of Paris since 1334. ▶ From the boulevard, view the monumental Louis XVI façade which glowers over the Cour du Mai — this is the main public entrance to the Law Courts of the Palais de Justice. Constant comings and goings of lawyers, magistrates, and people with nothing better to do ; tag along, and you will find yourself in the immense **Salle des Pas-Perdus**, the centre of the City's judicial life. Some of the courtrooms have retained fine elements of their original décor, notably the **Chambre Dorée★** (Gilded Chamber) where Marie-Antoinette was condemned to death. Original *boiseries*. ▶ By now, you will probably be surfeited with gold leaf, stucco and pompous allegories — so take the passage to the left of the Cour du Mai to the breathtakingly lovely **Sainte-Chapelle★★★**. This is a masterpiece of Gothic art, built by Saint-Louis between 1246 and 1248 to house the relic of Christ's Crown of Thorns. Here the two superimposed naves give an impression of airy lightness, almost of fragility. The higher of the two seems to be a reliquary in itself, a jewel-box suffused with filtered light from the 13th and 14thC stained-glass windows *(10-5)*. ▶ At the exit of the Palais de Justice, the Rue de Lutèce leads through to the **Flower Market★**, one of the most picturesque spots in Paris, with its charm heightened by the gloomy surroundings : on one side, the Commercial Tribunal ; on the other, the Hôtel Dieu (hospital) ; behind, the Préfecture de Police. ▶ From here, go back to the Place du Parvis-Notre-Dame and go down into the bizarre **Crypte Archéologique★** *(10-12, 2-6 daily);* exhibition of steles (inscribed upright stone slabs), reliefs, fragments of statues and inscriptions which bring to life the Paris-that-existed-before-Paris, when the Île de la Cité was merely the site of a small village. ▶ At the upstream end of the island, see the moving **Mémorial de la Déportation★★** (1962), commemorating those who were taken away to labour and concentration camps during World War II *(10-12 & 2-5 daily)*.   □

▶ CLUNY Museum**

Map 11-D6 / 6, Place Paul-Painlevé, 5th arr. Métro : Saint-Michel, Odéon, Maubert-Mutualité. RER : Saint-Michel. Bus : 21, 24, 27, 38, 63, 85, 86, 87, 96.

On the ruined thermal baths of Lutetia, built by the Seine boatmen's corporation in the 2nd or 3rdC, the 14thC Abbots of Cluny raised a luxury Paris residence for their own use. On the initiative of A. de Sommerard, a prominent collector and antiquarian, the present building (15thC Flamboyant Gothic) was converted into a museum in 1844.

▶ In the Museum's pleasant and well-lit rooms *(9:45-12:30/2-5:15; closed Tue.)* there is a fine exhibition of medieval ivories, reliquaries, altarpieces, toys and miscellaneous objects in gold. ▶ **Tapestries** are among the Cluny Museum's most important exhibits, especially the famous "Dame à la Licorne"★★ (15thC and rediscovered by George Sand) ; note also "La Vie Seigneuriale"★★ (16thC) and "L'Offrande du Cœur" (early 15thC). In addition, numerous 14th and 15thC statues. ▶ The large **Roman Pump Room★** (Salle des Thermes Romains) is the only Roman construction in France which still retains its original arches. Display of archaeological remains, including part of the "Pilier des Nautes", the most ancient sculpture in Paris. ☐

▶ COGNACQ-JAY Museum

Map 5-D4 / 25, Blvd. des Capucines, 2nd arr. Métro : Madeleine, Opéra. Bus : 20, 21, 27, 29, 42, 52, 53, 66, 68, 95.

Ernest Cognacq, founder of the La Samaritaine group of stores, created this museum of 18thC France in collaboration with his wife, Louise Jay. It was opened in 1929, foreshadowing the appearance of thorough American-style foundations endowed by private collectors. The Cognacq-Jay Museum contains *boiseries,* precious objects, furniture, porcelain and miniatures, harmonizing perfectly with paintings (Boucher, Chardin, Fragonard) and drawings (Watteau). Nothing is overdone or dull on any of the three floors ; the impression is of constant decorative perfection and refinement, the hallmark of the great century of French taste *(10-5:40 ; closed Mon.).* ☐

▶ Place de la CONCORDE★★★

Map 9-C4 / 8th arr. Métro : Concorde. Bus : 24, 42, 52, 72, 73, 84, 94.

The Concorde is at the crossroads of two magnificent vistas : the Tuileries to the Champs-Élysées, and the Madeleine to the Palais Bourbon. It is also the largest unencumbered urban space in Paris.

▶ The Place de la Concorde owes its existence to the aldermen of Paris, who commissioned an equestrian statue of Louis XV and began to look for a place to put it ; this the king supplied in 1759 by entrusting Gabriel with the reclamation of a marshy area close to the Tuileries. The architect conceived the Place Louis XV to match the surroundings, built the Ambassador's Mansions (now the Hôtel Crillon and the Navy Ministry) and surrounded the square with an octagonal moat which has now been filled in. The square was inaugurated in 1763. During the Revolution, the statue of Louis XV was removed and replaced by the guillotine, and the Place de la Concorde was confirmed in its present name under the July Monarchy. Louis-Philippe, who wished at all costs to avoid any political symbolism, erected the pink granite obelisk★ that stands there today, a gift from the government of Egypt in 1831. ▶ This obelisk was originally taken from the Temple of Rameses II at Thebes ; it stands 23 metres high and is covered with hieroglyphs. Two high fountains play around its base. On the perimeter of the square are eight allegorical statues of the great towns of France. Where the Avenue des Champs-Élysées joins the Place de la Concorde you can see the famous rearing horses (Chevaux de Marly★★, 1719) by Coustou, installed here in 1795. At the Tuileries entrance are Coysevox's equestrian statues. ☐

▶ La DÉFENSE★

Map p. 58-59 A1, 60 / Pont de Neuilly, Puteaux. Métro : Pont de Neuilly ; RER : La Défense. Bus : 73.

La Défense was originally designed some fifteen years ago as a kind of Paris Manhattan, built in the old quarters of Puteaux, Nanterre and Courbevoie.

▶ La Défense has its commercial centre, exhibition halls (Palais des Expositions★ - Centre National des Industries et des Techniques) and headquarters of giant companies. But of late it has also become a pleasant place to walk about. The areas around the skyscraper towers have been converted to pedestrian precincts, and special efforts have been made to maintain an atmosphere of constant animation. This is supplied by the *CNIT's* exhibitions (computer science, domestic arts, boat show, children's show, etc.), along with jazz and classical music concerts in summer. There are also art exhibitions open to young artists.   □

Le Métro

On the 19th of July 1900, after only two years of work, the first line on the Metropolitan railway (designed by the government engineer Fulgence Bienvenüe) was inaugurated. Some Métro entrances still date from the turn of the century; conceived by Hector Guimard, they are characteristic of what was known as the "modern style" — Art Nouveau. By 1945, the network covered 145 km; nowadays it has reached nearly 200 km, with no less than 280 stations, and a number of suburban extensions under construction or at the planning stage. Every day, the Métro's 3500 carriages carry over 4 million travelers with clockwork reliability. The Express Regional Network (RER), operated jointly by the SNCF (National Railway Company) and the RATP (Paris Transport Network) connects the outlying Île-de-France region with the heart of the capital.

▶ EIFFEL TOWER***

Map 8-A5 / 7th arr. Métro : Bir-Hakeim. RER : Champ-de-Mars. Bus : 42, 69, 82, 87.

Everything has been said, and more, about this "superstar" of Paris tourist attractions, which attracts no less than 3 million visitors each year. The Universal Exhibition of 1889 instigated the building of an iron tower, as a symbol of the triumph of industrial civilization. Gustave Eiffel, an engineer and specialist in metal construction techniques, was chosen from 700 other competitors to make this idea a reality. The work lasted from January 1887 until the spring of 1889; 7000 metric tonnes of iron, two and a half million rivets, 320 metres high... the figures make you dizzy, but perhaps the most astonishing fact of all is that not a single correction was made to the plans during construction, so perfect was Eiffel's final design.

▶ The Eiffel Tower today serves, apart from a favourite subject for painters, as a meteorological station and radio mast; every day its three levels are visited by thousands of people *(9:30 am-11 pm daily for the first and second levels, 9:30-8 daily for the top level)*. Those who go straight to the summit are sometimes disappointed by clouds which obscure the stunning panorama★★★ over Paris; on cloudy days, therefore, the best view is to be had from the second level. Other, taller towers have been built in New York, Moscow and elsewhere. Nevertheless, this old lady of nearly a hundred, who bears her age lightly under forty tons of paint, still retains her power to fascinate.   □

▶ FAUBOURG SAINT-GERMAIN*

Map 9-C5 / 7th arr. Métro : Invalides, Varennes, Chambres-des-Députés, Solférino, Rue-du-Bac. RER : Quai d'Orsay. Bus : 28, 49, 63, 69, 83, 84, 87, 94.

Between the Seine, the Invalides and the Boulevard Saint-Germain lies an elegant quarter which was first inhabited towards the end of the 17thC. As a result, the Faubourg Saint-Germain is a kind of life-size museum of the civil architecture which predominated in that era. On the site of an old game preserve, large numbers of fine houses were constructed in the early 18thC, which later became the homes of important functionaries and rich bourgeois during the Empire, before being turned into an immense complex of embassies and government ministries. Most were built along the same lines : two symmetrical façades enclosing a courtyard, which opens on the street through a decorated gateway. The main part of the building faces in the other direction, onto a park dotted with pavilions, balusters and fountains.

▶ The only two buildings here which are open to the public are the **Hôtel Biron★,** now the Rodin Museum, and the **Hôtel de Salm★** (1782, Museum of the Legion of Honour, 2 Rue de Bellechasse, *2-5; closed Mon.*). However, if you take a walk beginning at the antique shops and art galleries of the Quai Voltaire, taking in Rue du Bac, Rue de Beaune and Rue des Saints-Pères, you can get a sight of the *hôtels* of the **Rue de l'Université** (Nos. 17, 33, 60 and the Hôtel de Soyécourt★, 1707, No. 51), then the *hôtels* of the **Rue St-Dominique** (Hôtel de Brienne, No. 14 ; Hôtel de Broglie, No. 35 ; Hôtel de Sagan★, 1715, No. 57). Continue to the Quatre Saisons★ (Four Seasons) Fountain at No. 57, **Rue de Grenelle,** which leads to a group of 18thC houses (Nos. 70, 85, 87, 106-120, 140, 142). On either side of the **Hôtel Matignon** (1720), which is the Prime Minister's residence, the **Rue de Varenne** offers the Hôtel de Boisgelin★ (Italian Embassy), and other *hôtels* at Nos. 45, 47, 50, 56, 60, 73 and 75. At the end of the Rue de Bourgogne stands the **Palais-Bourbon★,** now the Chamber of Deputies. This building dates from 1722, and was enlarged by the addition of the **Hôtel de Lassay★★,** a palace decorated with a number of allegories and statues. Frescoes by Eugène Delacroix in the library.   □

▶ FAUBOURG SAINT-HONORÉ*

Map 4-C4 / 8th arr. Métro : St-Philippe-du-Roule. Bus : 28, 32, 42, 49, 52, 80, 83.

Between the Place Beauvau and the Rue Royale runs the Faubourg Saint-Honoré, which lays serious claim to be the international capital of *haute-couture* and luxury commerce.

▶ Distinguished residences, built in the early 18thC by financiers and businessmen of the period, punctuate the succession of boutiques : in the main, these are now foreign embassies. The British Embassy★ is at No. 39, in Pauline (Bonaparte) Borghese's former town house, amid a cluster of early 18thC mansions in various states of preservation. On the Place Beauvau, the *hôtel* built around 1760 for the Comte de Beauvau is now occupied by the Ministry of the Interior ; but the Faubourg's best-known address is unquestionably No. 55-57 — the **Élysée Palace★★,** which originally belonged to the Count of Évreux and later, Madame de Pompadour, became a public dance-hall during the Revolution, and is now (since 1873) the residence of the President of the French Republic.   □

▶ GRAND PALAIS, PETIT PALAIS*

Map 4-B4 / Petit Palais : Avenue Winston-Churchill. Grand Palais : Avenue Winston-Churchill, Avenue de Selves and Avenue Franklin-Roosevelt, 8th arr. Métro : Champs-Élysées-Clemenceau. Bus : 28, 42, 49, 72, 73, 83.

The Grand Palais and Petit Palais stand on the site of the 1900 Universal Exhibition, where marvels from the four corners of the earth were displayed ; one of the most talked-about was the moving walkway that circled the pavilions.

▶ The **Grand Palais** was for many years the accustomed venue for Paris's great commercial exhibitions. The huge facilities at the Porte de Versailles and La Défense have now taken over this function, and the Grand Palais is now devoted to art shows *(10-8 daily, 10-10 Wed.; closed Tue.).* The gigantic glass roof★★ which covers the hall is a masterpiece of Art Nouveau iron architecture. ▶ Behind the Grand Palais, on the Avenue Franklin-Roosevelt, is the **Palais de la Découverte**★★ *(10-6, closed Mon. and nat. hols.),* displaying the various discoveries of modern science; interesting for both children and adults. Popularization of knowledge is the rule here; the major attraction, a **planetarium,** offers a scaled-down version of the night sky, with 9000 stars swimming slowly across it. ▶ The **Petit Palais** has now been transformed into a **Fine Arts Museum★** by the City of Paris. It presents highly diverse collections relative to France in the 19thC : paintings by Delacroix, Géricault, Courbet, Monet, and Cézanne, along with a number of objects from the turn of the century. Also fine antiques and 18thC furniture. Frequent temporary exhibitions *(10-5:40; closed Mon.).* □

▶ The GRANDS BOULEVARDS

Map 5-D4 / 1st, 2nd, 3rd, 8th, 9th and 10th arrs. Métro : Madeleine, Opéra, Richelieu-Drouot, Bonne-Nouvelle, Strasbourg-St-Denis. Bus : 20, 21, 22, 24, 27, 29, 38, 39, 42, 47, 48, 52, 67, 85, 95.

▶ The **Boulevard de la Madeleine** and the **Boulevard des Capucines,** between the *Café de la Paix, Fauchon* and the Trois Quartiers department store, still maintain a certain tradition of luxury, even though the beautiful professional *marcheuses* (streetwalkers) of former times no longer walk here to disturb the serenity of Parisian males. ▶ Behind the Opéra, the **Boulevard Haussmann** becomes thoroughly dreary once it has passed the big department stores *(Grands Magasins)* and the vicinity of the St. Lazare railway station. The **Boulevard Malesherbes** peters out in the monotonously genteel 17th arrondissement. ▶ The real Grands Boulevards, which in the 19thC made a fine promenade all the way to the Place de la République, have now been wholly stripped of their original character by the proliferation of fast-food shops, couscous restaurants and other such establishments. ▶ Close by is the business quarter, huddled round the **Bourse★** (Stock Exchange), a somewhat severe Corinthian temple designed by Brongniart in 1825. This district passes into a deep sleep as soon as the offices close down in the evening, in contrast to the adjacent **Strasbourg-St. Denis** neighbourhood which seethes with lovers of Kung-Fu and pornographic movies. There is nothing especially Parisian about the crowds of tourists and seekers of doubtful pleasures around the **Porte St. Denis** and **Porte St. Martin,** but the *quartier* does still have one or two fine 19thC buildings such as the Porte St. Martin Theatre (1829), the Gymnase Theatre (38 Blvd. de Bonne-Nouvelle, 1820), the Variety Theatre (7 Blvd. Montmartre, 1807) and, coming back towards the Opéra, the **Opéra-Comique** (Blvd. des Italiens) or the **Maison Dorée,** on the corner of the Rue Laffitte (1839). □

▶ GUIMET Museum*

Map 8-A4 / 6, Place d'Iéna, 16th arr. Métro : Iéna. Bus : 32, 63, 82.

The industrialist, musician and traveler Émile Guimet left his collections of Far-Eastern art to the state when he died in 1884. Today they form the core of the newly renovated Guimet Museum, one of the richest exhibitions of Asiatic art on the planet *(9:45-12/ 1:30-5:15; closed Tue. and nat. hols.).*

▶ Impressive **Cambodian statues★** at the museum's entrance set a religious tone that pervades most of the Cambodian and Southeast Asian works exhibited here, spanning the 6th to the 13thC. The contrast between these idealized and often enigmatic pieces and the **decorative objects** from Pakistan, Afghanistan and India, emphasizes the myriad influences affecting this crossroads between East and West. The 11thC Dancing Shiva★, the Flower Spirit with its Greek overtones, and the 2ndC King of the Snakes are among the greatest masterpieces of the Indian subcontinent. For those who don't care for bronzes, hundred-armed goddesses and painted banners, there is the sumptuous collection of **porcelain and ceramics★★★**, which is unrivaled anywhere in the world for its sheer decorative richness, variety of subject matter, and exquisite craftsmanship.   □

▶ Les HALLES*

Map 11-E5 / 1st arr. Métro : Châtelet-Les Halles, Étienne-Marcel. RER : Châtelet-Les Halles. Bus : 21, 29, 38, 47, 58, 67, 69, 70, 72, 74, 81, 85.

Les Halles are dead ; long live Les Halles ! The "Ventre de Paris" ("The Belly of Paris") from the 12thC on, the great Halles food and flower market in Baltard's glass-and-metal pavilions at the centre of Paris had been slowly suffocating in an everlasting traffic jam. It continued to do so until the 1970s when the markets were moved to Rungis, well out of town on the main road to Orly Airport. Now the *quartier* is focused on a gigantic crater, where the markets used to stand — the largest urban project attempted in Paris since the Baron Haussmann, and the superb **Fountain of Innocents★★**, a 1549 Renaissance masterpiece by Jean Goujon.

▶ Today's Les Halles is an underground labyrinth, built over a railway station which is itself 25 metres below the surface. It includes some five thousand metres of streets and theatres, the **Grévin Museum** *(10:30-6:45, Sun. and hols. 1-7:15),* and a **shopping forum★** filled with boutiques, stores and cinemas around a series of lively arcades. The forum is the work of two architects, Vasconi and Penchréac'h, who have taken care that abundant light should penetrate all four underground levels ; glass arches, symbolizing the modern Halles, echo the stone arches of the **church of Saint-Eustache** opposite (→), which represent Medieval and Renaissance Paris. Do not miss the **Holographie Museum** on level 1, 15-21 Grand Balcon *(11-7, Sun. and hols. 1-7).* ▶ On the corner of Rues Pierre-Lescot and Rambuteau, the municipality has created a **cultural centre** housing studios, exhibition halls, poetry workshop (Maison de la Poésie) and, above all, a cultural information service (SVP Culturel) supplying information from a computer bank. ▶ An underground district connecting Saint-Eustache, the Bourse and the Forum, **l'Espace des Halles** offers athletic, educational, social and, above all, cultural activities : **l'Espace photographique de Paris,** photo exhibits and archives open to the public ; the **Maison des Conservatoires,** meeting point for Paris music, dance and theatre conservatories ; an **auditorium** that seats 600 and a **discothèque ;** green spaces such as the **serre panoramique** (greenhouse) displaying 72 plant varieties on 450 square meters, and a 50 m-long **swimming pool** in an elegant setting. ▶ Apartments, a day-nursery and a garden which extends as far as the **Bourse du Commerce** (Commercial Stock Exchange) complete the setting, which is a popular meeting place for the young and the old avant-garde, as well as for artists, marginals and aggressive hooligans.   □

▶ HÔTEL DE VILLE

Map 11-E5 / Place de l'Hôtel-de-Ville, 4th arr. Métro : Hôtel-de-Ville. Bus : 38, 47, 58, 67, 69, 70, 72, 74, 75, 76, 96.

The Hôtel de Ville, headquarters of the mayor's administration, celebrated its centenary in 1982. This occasion was marked by a refurbishment of the former Place de Grève, now the Place de l'Hôtel-de-Ville, which stands in front. This pedestrians-only square was the setting for public executions in the Middle Ages; nowadays it shimmers with flowers and fountains, and below the surface is a huge car park.

▶ The history of the Mairie de Paris (Municipal Authority) goes back to the reign of St. Louis, who in 1260 demanded of the people of Paris that they designate a Provost *(Prévôt)* and Aldermen. The latter deliberated in a salt-merchant's house on the Place de Grève, known as the "Parloir aux Bourgeois". A century later, in 1357, Provost Étienne Marcel bought the "Maison aux Piliers" on behalf of the City of Paris; subsequently greatly enlarged, first under François I, then during the July Monarchy, the building was totally demolished during the revolt of the Commune on the 24th of May 1871, then rebuilt according to a design by Ballu. ▶ The ornate façade of the Hôtel de Ville, with its Renaissance-style statues and decorations, was, for many years, roundly abused by Parisians; nowadays it is recognized for what it is, one of the greatest monuments of the 19thC. The ceremonial rooms inside (sumptuous, but highly impractical) now draw most of the critics' fire. *(Group visits, by request : Accueil de la Ville de Paris, 49, rue de Rivoli.)*   □

▶ INSTITUT**

Map 10-D5 / Quai Conti, 6th arr. Métro : Saint-Germain, Pont-Neuf. Bus : 24, 27, 39, 48, 58, 70, 95.

Under the Institut's august dome, the academicians brood over their interminable dictionary of the French language. Here also the hallowed sages of science and the arts meet in the learned assemblies of the Academy's five branches : Literature, Science, Fine Arts, Moral and Political Science.

▶ These five academies all occupy the serene **Palais de l'Institut de France★★,** designed by Louis Le Vau and completed after his death in 1691 by Lambert and d'Orbay. Before becoming the seat of the French Academy (founded by Richelieu in 1635), this building was occupied by the Collège des Quatre-Nations, as decreed by Cardinal Mazarin — who also bequeathed it his library. The present Bibliothèque Mazarine★ possesses more than 5 000 000 volumes, manuscripts and precious incunabula, stored in its premises in the Tour de Nesle *(10-6; closed Sat. and Sun.).* Students and scholars now work in this tower, from which Queen Margot is said to have had her nightly lovers flung into the Seine. ▶ Close by, on the Quay, stands the **Hôtel de la Monnaie★** (Mint, 1771-77), a fine example of Louis XVI architecture (striking of medals ; medal displays ; *11-6; closed Mon.*).   □

Unusual museums :
Musée de l'Assistance publique

The Public Health Museum, in a fine 17thC aristocratic mansion : a display of ten centuries of medical history, bizarre instruments, anecdotes and curiosities. (47 Quai de la Tournelle, 5th arr. 10-5; closed Mon, Tue. and hols.).

▶ INSTITUT DU MONDE ARABE
(Arab World Institute)

Map 11-E6 / 5th arr. Métro : Gare d'Austerlitz, Jussieu.

Until recently the centre for Islamic culture was contained in the prestigious **Institut des études musul-**

manes across from the Jardin des Plantes (Botanical Gardens). The Institut du Monde Arabe, established by France and nineteen Arab countries, is the new cultural headquarters for an Islamic art and civilization museum, a library with over 40 000 works and an antenna for cultural programming. □

▶ Les INVALIDES***

Map 9-B5 / 7th arr. Métro : Invalides, Varenne, Latour-Maubourg. RER : Invalides. Bus : 28, 49, 63, 69, 82, 83, 92.

Les Invalides testifies to the military grandeur of France under the Empire and the post-revolutionary Republic. The facade, perhaps the finest in Paris, gives onto a majestic lawn-covered esplanade extending all the way to the banks of the Seine. It was Louis XIV, the Sun King, who announced (in the edicts of 1670 and 1674) the creation of Les Invalides as a home for wounded veterans of his armies.

▶ Les Invalides is the work of two successive architects, Libéral Bruant and Hardouin-Mansart. The latter was responsible for the monumental general design of the building, especially the remarkable **dome★★** on the Place Vauban side, which took 25 years to build (1679-1706). ▶ A more fitting imperial mausoleum could scarcely be conceived for the **tomb of Napoleon I★**, which has lain in the crypt here since 1840 *(10-5 daily, 10-7 Jul.-Aug.)* when the ex-Emperor's body was brought back in triumph from St. Helena. His ashes are contained in six coffins inside an ornate red porphyry monument. Visitors file past in the golden half-light of the crypt, their minds no doubt filled with memories of Austerlitz and Waterloo... ▶ It is almost impossible to visit all of Les Invalides, with its 16 km of corridors. After the obligatory visit to the Dôme church, the royal church, the next stop should be the **church of St. Louis-des-Invalides★**, used by the soldiers. Once again, the former military splendours of France are evoked : tombs of great generals, Napoleonic memorabilia, remains of no less than 1 417 standards captured from assorted enemies. The somewhat less warlike 17thC organ is one of the most beautiful in Paris. ▶ The two buildings of the **Musée de l'Armée★★** (Army Museum ; *10-5 or 6 according to season*) enclose the courtyard. ▶ Lost in the garrets of the Invalides are the remarkable and most interesting **Plans-Reliefs★** (relief maps). Here are 1/600 scale models of great cities and fortresses in France and abroad, ranging from Louis XIV to Napoleon III. □

▶ JARDIN DES PLANTES*
(Botanical Gardens)

Map 11-F6 / 5th arr. Entrances : Place Buffon, Place Valhubert. Métro : Jussieu, Place Monge, Gare d'Austerlitz. RER : Gare d'Austerlitz. Bus : 24, 57, 61, 63, 65, 89, 91.

Created by Louis XIII as a "royal medicinal herb garden", and developed by the naturalists Fagon, Jussieu and (especially) Buffon, the Jardin des Plantes is today a haunt of children, students from the vicinity and retired people who wander under the aged trees or around the pits and aviaries of the zoo. In the 18thC this place was a centre for the fashionable aristocratic study of botany.

▶ Galleries devoted to mineralogy, entomology, palaeobotany, palaeontology and comparative anatomy... these names may make you a trifle languid, but the main gallery of the **Museum of Natural History★★** has a magic of its own, with its armies of skeletons and resplendent collections of minerals and butterflies. Some of the greatest names in world biology (Buffon, Daubenton, Cuvier) worked in this museum ; nonetheless, it became one of the poorest on earth, though its collections are among the richest. Now it has been renovated and restored, and at last can display its possessions in fit surroundings (57, rue Cuvier, *1:30-5; closed Tue. and nat. hols.*). □

▶ LATIN QUARTER

Map 10-D5 / 5th and 6th arrs. Métro : Odéon, Saint-Michel, Maubert. RER : Luxembourg. Bus : 21, 24, 27, 38, 47, 58, 63, 67, 70, 84, 85, 86, 87, 89, 96.

From the **Odéon Theatre★** to the "heretical" skyscraper of the Faculty of Sciences (Jussieu), from the Place St-Michel to the Rue Mouffetard, the uniting factor for the Latin Quarter has been the Sorbonne. In the 12thC, Abélard rebelled against the ecclesiastical teachings of the Île de la Cité, and his students followed him across the river to found a new university ; subsequently, in 1253, Robert de Sorbon opened a college which offered room and board to poor students. His name was extended to cover an institution grouping no less than four universities on the Left Bank, and the 10 000 students who flocked to the Sorbonne made Paris the intellectual capital of Christendom. Among the most renowned teachers here were St. Bonaventure, Albert le Grand, St. Thomas Aquinas and Malebranche. The Sorbonne was always a turbulent community, opposed to the royal authority ; and by 1792 it had declined almost to the point of no return. Napoleon I breathed new life into it, but it was not until the Third Republic that a modern university was established, which the events of May 1968 fragmented into 13 multi-disciplinary universities scattered all over Paris and the suburbs. From the Carrefour de l'Odéon, one continues to the **Place Saint-Sulpice★★,** shaded by chestnut trees. In the centre is the monumental Fountain of the Four Bishops (1844), while to the E is the **Saint-Sulpice church★,** typical of the 17th and 18thC Classical style with a reference to Antiquity *à la* Palladio. Sarvandoni undertook the famous façade whose towers were reworked by Chalgrin. Inside, statues by Bouchardon, Pigalle ; paintings by C. Van Loo and especially, the **chapelle des anges★** (angel's chapel, *1st on right*), decorated by Delacroix and on which he worked until his death in 1863.

▶ The Latin Quarter is today divided up by the Haussmann **boulevards of St-Michel** and **St-Germain.** Historically, its main artery was the **Rue St-Jacques,** which follows the lie of an old Gallo-Roman road. ▶ The Boulevard St-Michel, 1.5 km long, begins at Davioud's amazing Second Empire **fountain,** at the centre of the Place St-Michel and for years a great rallying point for Paris marginals. The latter have been drummed off the café terraces of the **St. André-des-Arts** and **îlot St. Séverin★** *quartier* by the progressive commercial banality of these ancient streets (fine 18thC houses★ at No. 29, Rue de la Parcheminerie, Rue de la Harpe, odd numbers, Rues des Grands-Augustins, Séguier, Gît-le-Cœur ; also Nos. 47 and 52, Rue St-André-des-Arts). ▶ The atmosphere becomes duller in proportion to the growing number of boutiques ; around the Sorbonne, however, a few "experimental" cinemas and bookshops maintain a token student presence. The **Sorbonne** itself, a gigantic barrack dating from 1900, deploys its 22 lecture theatres and scores of classrooms around a series of decorated corridors (frescoes and "kitsch" allegories). The main lecture theatre was embellished by Puvis de Chavannes. The only ancient part is the elegant **chapel★** (by Lemercier, 1635) with its domed façade dominating the Place de la Sorbonne. Inside, paintings by Philippe de Champaigne and Richelieu's tomb, by Girardon. ▶ **The Collège de France** on the Place Marcellin-Berthelot is dedicated to the impartial study of arts and sciences. The first stone of this building was laid by Louis XIII, though it was not completed

until 1780. ▶ On the top of the "Montagne" Sainte-Geneviève, by the **Place du Panthéon** (→), the church of Saint-
Étienne-du-Mont★★ is dedicated to Geneviève, the saint
who saved Paris (late 15thC; choir-screen, tombs of Pascal and Racine). Also the **Sainte-Geneviève Library,** with
1 700 000 volumes. The **Lycée Henri IV** (school) unfortunately bars the access to the remains of the Romanesque
abbey of Sainte-Geneviève (kitchens, refectory, tower of
Clovis, Library). ▶ The **Place de la Contrescarpe,** behind
the Lycée Henri IV, is very lively at night, with a mixture
of tramps, students and tourists. Innumerable restaurants
and their cosmopolitan clientele are gradually forcing out
the traditional inhabitants, who nowadays only manage to
get together in the mornings for the provincial market★★
at the bottom of the **Rue Mouffetard.** ▶ The "Mouffe" is
now an upscale neighbourhood but has managed to keep
the feeling of a protected outpost, especially around the
church of Saint-Médard★. This curious sanctuary is a
blend of Flamboyant Gothic, Renaissance, 17thC and the
fashionable Antique style of the 18thC.   □

▶ The LOUVRE***

Map 10-D5 / 1st arr. Métro : Louvre, Palais-Royal. Bus :
21, 24, 27, 39, 48, 67, 69, 72, 74, 76, 81, 85, 95.

Seen from the Seine or the Tuileries Gardens, the largest building complex in Paris gives a false impression of unity; this is not far short of miraculous, since
the Louvre took no less than eight centuries to reach
its present state.

▶ First, the square fortress built by Philippe Auguste
(1190), and Etienne Marcel's ramparts; then the "library"
of Charles V, the château begun by Pierre Lescot for
François I and Henri II, which was carried on by Catherine de Médicis and Henri IV; then the finishing work
done by Louis XIV. After this came the museum installed
by the Revolution, which was enlarged under Napoléon;
the 1871 burning of the Tuileries by the Communards;
and finally André Malraux's restoration of the original
moats (filled in during the transformation from fortress to
palace) in 1965. The Louvre has never ceased to adapt
and change. The current challenge is its "Grand Louvre"
projet, directed by the Chinese-born American architect
I. M. Pei. Its first step is the construction of a transparent
pyramid at the entrance to the museum. Then it will reno-
vate the interior of the Ministry of France offices. ▶ The
Vieux (Old) Louvre (1660-80) with its famous **colon-
nade**★★ facing the Place du Louvre, surrounds the **Cour
Carrée** (Square Courtyard)★ and continues along the
Seine as far as the Pont du Carrousel. The W wing of the
Cour Carrée is older; this structure is a masterpiece of
the French Renaissance, with superb pediments. ▶ The
Nouveau (New) Louvre spreads its wings as far as the
Pont du Carrousel; its construction dates partly from
Napoléon III and partly from the Third Republic, after
the burning of the Tuileries (Flore and Marsan Pavilions).
Between these two galleries, the gardens are dotted with
Maillol's nude statues★, much beloved by photographers.

The Louvre in detail

▶ The **Louvre Museum** is situated in the "Vieux Louvre"
around the Cour Carrée (Square Courtyard) and the section of the former palace that follows the Seine *(9:45-5:15
or 6:30, according to the zone; museum fully open Mon.
and Wed.; closed Tue., tel. : 42.86.99.00).* It seems futile
to attempt any kind of resumé of the Louvre's fabulous collections, of which the small proportion on view
to the public is already enough to fill dozens and dozens
of immense exhibition rooms. The best way to see the
Louvre is the following : spend a half day looking over the
principal masterpieces, and then come again in the days
following to concentrate exclusively on certain departments. There are six of these, grouping objects broadly
according to family. ▶ The **Ancient Greek** and **Roman
pieces** *(ground floor)* which have recently been reorganized, are headed by the famous **Winged Victory of
Samothrace,** which was discovered in 1863. This statue

stands at the top of a majestic staircase along with the armless **Venus de Milo**, originally a gift to Louis XVIII. The "Venus" dates from the 2ndC BC. In a special room adjoining are several pieces from the Parthenon, notably the Panathenian Frieze. Roman sculpture achieved an apotheosis with the creation of the Barbarian Princes and the Apollo. ▶ Once known as the "Assyrian Museum", the department of **Oriental Antiquities** *(ground floor, Cour Carrée)* displays treasures from the Near East : the Code of Hammurabi, a basalt stone bearing the laws of Babylon (1750 B.C.) ; Frieze of Archers, representing the King of Persia's bowmen (6thC BC) ; and statue of the Commissary (intendant) Ebih-II, from the 3rd millennium BC, with eyes seeming to gaze on eternity. ▶ The **Ancient Egypt section** *(ground floor, basement and first floor, Cour Carrée)* has benefited from the prodigious discoveries made by Champollion and Marielle. Wide variety of figurines and jewelry ; also statues like the colossal Sphinx and the famous Seated Scribe. Fine sarcophagi and steles, along with an entirely reconstructed Mastaba, or funeral chamber. ▶ **The Objets d'Art and Furniture department** *(1st floor, Cour Carrée)* offers an eclectic collection of furniture and objects from the Middle Ages to the 19thC. These include Roman reliquaries, ivories, enamelling, and snuff boxes. It would take hours and hours to give each object here the attention it deserves. Notice especially the lovely Boulle furniture ; Marie Leszczynska's dressing case, given to her in 1729 ; and, in the **Apollo Gallery★★★**, the **Crown Jewels** with the astonishing 137-carat "Regent" Diamond, acquired by Philippe d'Orléans in 1717. ▶ The **Paintings section** is perhaps the best known part of the Louvre. *(1st floor, Grande Galerie, Aile de Flore, etc. 9:45-5, closed Tue.).* It seems to be perpetually undergoing reorganization and contains works covering the development of European painting, from the 14th to the 19thC. **French painting** is represented by such masterpieces as the *Pietà* d'Avignon, Watteau's *Gilles* and Poussin's *Bergers d'Arcadie.* Nonetheless, the public seems to prefer works by the Italian masters, headed by Leonardo's *Mona Lisa* ("La Joconde" in French), a veritable superstar. This mysterious painting tends to overshadow Leonardo's other works in the Louvre, *The Virgin of the Rocks* and *The Virgin, the Child Jesus and Saint Anne,* but it should not distract too much attention from the lovely creations of Fra Angelico, Uccello, Titian and Raphael hanging nearby. The **Flemish and Dutch masters** offer a considerable contrast in style, represented by Van Eyck, Memling, Rubens, Rembrandt and above all, the fascinating Vermeer, to whose *Lacemaker (Dentellière)* has now been added *The Astronomer* from the Rothschild collection. Lastly, the **Cabinet des Dessins** (Drawings department) offers constantly rotating exhibitions from its stock of 80 000 drawings. ▶ **Sculpture** is the last and perhaps the least-visited of the Louvre's sections ; nonetheless, it contains Michelangelo's famous *Slaves* along with important works by Donatello, Jean Goujon, Germain Pilon and Carpeaux.□

▶ LUXEMBOURG Gardens and Palace**

Map 10-D6 / 6th arr. RER : Luxembourg. Bus : 21, 27, 38, 58, 82, 84, 85, 89.

The Luxembourg Gardens, once so beloved of Marie de Médicis, is a peaceful spot for the horticulturists to work on the orchids (more than 400 varieties) of the Orangerie, and the gardens' orchards.

▶ After the assassination of Henri IV, his widow, Marie de Médicis, began building a palace (1615) in the gardens she had recently bought from François de Luxembourg and to which she constantly added. ▶ On the Rue de Tournon side, the Palace★★, designed by Salomon de Brosse, retains its original Florentine features. The building now houses the French Senate and was considerably modified in the 19thC. Haussmann was only prevented from destroying the Park by a petition signed by 12 000 people : as it was, the building of the Rue Auguste-

Comte reduced it to its present 60-odd acres. ▶ The Luxembourg is above all a highly civilized park, with its ponds, its terraces, its pretty Fontaine Médicis and its monument to Delacroix. Though it has lost its chair-attendants, the chairs are still there; alas, the park wardens are implacable about the hour of closing, which is exactly thirty minutes before sunset at all times of year. From the Luxembourg Gardens by the Avenue de l'Observatoire or the Rue Gay-Lussac one reaches the Boulevard Port-Royal and the **Val-de-Grâce** military hospital★★ : the former monastery founded by Anne d'Autriche is one of the most remarkable architectural ensembles of the 17thC. Built to the design of F. Mansart, the dome is one of the finest examples of Roman Baroque in Paris.   □

▶ Church of La MADELEINE

Map 4-C4 / Place de la Madeleine, 8th arr. Metro : Madeleine. Bus : 24, 42, 52, 84, 94.

The majestic, slightly ponderous Church of the Madeleine, with its temple facade and its perron 24 steps high, is very much in tune with its smart location at the top of the Rue Royale. This is the core of Paris's luxury commercial area and the crux of the Grands Boulevards.

▶ The church was begun by Napoléon I who wanted a temple dedicated to his Grand Army; but it was not completed until 1840.   □

▶ Château de MALMAISON*** and de BOIS-PRÉAU*

R.E.R. : Rueil-Malmaison (Line A).

A temporary residence of Napoléon during the Consulate, and later, Empress Josephine's retreat, Malmaison and its "annex", the Bois-Préau, offer a marvelous example of Empire-style decoration : furniture, paintings, memorabilia *(10-12 & 1:30-4:30 or 5)*. In the **park★,** rose garden. ▶ 3 km S. : ponds of Saint-Cucufa.   □

▶ The MARAIS***

Map 12-F5 / 3rd and 4th arr. Métro : Saint-Paul, Pont-Marie *(S side)*, Bastille, Chemin-Vert, Rambuteau *(N side)*. Bus : 20, 29, 38, 47, 65, 67, 69, 75, 76, 86, 87, 91, 96.

The twisting streets, magnificent private mansions, courtyards and ancient buildings of the Marais quarter cover some 300 acres of protected *(classé)* townscape. This *quartier* is really a huge museum of Paris, a living testimonial to the civil architecture of the 17thC. Not so long ago, it was on the brink of crumbling into ruin, but was saved *in extremis* by the Malraux Law of 1962, which led to a long and ultimately fruitful renovation of the Marais' forgotten treasures. Twenty years later, in the 1980s, accommodation here has become much sought after by wealthy Parisians just as it was in the days of Henri IV when aristocrats and burgers clustered around the Place Royale — now the Place des Vosges — and built themselves houses to match their wealth and ambition. The area is now considerably enlarged, stretching from the Church of St. Gervais to the Bastille and from the Seine to the Temple.

▶ The S end of the Marais between Rue St-Antoine and the Seine is typical of old Paris. The church of **St. Gervais-St. Protais★** (16thC, pure Flamboyant Gothic), is a good starting point for a visit to this side of the quar-

ter; its Classical façade (1620) stands right behind the
Hôtel de Ville. It was in this church that a German shell
killed 51 people on Good Friday, 1918. ▶ Continuing down
the **Rue François-Miron,** lovely houses of the precinct of
St. Gervais (1732 : Nos. 2-14). No. 68 on this street is the
Hôtel de Beauvais★ (1655); No. 82, the Hôtel du Pési-
dent Hénault (1706). ▶ To the right is Rue de Fourcy,
then Rue des Nonains-d'Hyeres; on the right, **Hôtel
d'Aumont★★** (1648); left, the rear façade of the **Hôtel de
Sens★★,** heavily restored but still a fine example of
15thC architecture. This *hôtel* was the home of the eccen-
tric Queen Margot; today, it houses the **Forney Library**
(1:30-8; closed Sun. and Mon.). ▶ Close by the Quai des
Célestins, a part of **Philippe Auguste's city wall** (1180) is
still visible (Rue des Jardins-Saint-Paul). ▶ At the end of
the quai is the Hôtel Fieubet, built by Mansart in 1678 but
loaded with superfluous additions in the 19thC; likewise
the mansion at No. 3 Rue de Sully, now occupied by the
Library of the Arsenal. This building still retains some
rooms decorated in the style of Louis XIII, unchanged
since the great finance minister Sully lived here *(10-5
daily; closed Sun.)* ▶ Via Rue du Petit-Musc, to the
ancient and busily commercial **Rue St-Antoine,** the central artery of the Marais. At No. 17, the circular **Temple of
St. Marie★,** built by Mansart in 1634; at No. 21, the Hôtel
de Mayenne (1613) and the exceptionally graceful **Hôtel
de Sully★★** at No. 62, built by Henri IV's great minister
in 1624; today, beautifully restored, this building houses
the Historic Monuments Board (C.N.M.H.S. → museums;
information centre). Next to the Lycée Charlemagne, fur-
ther on, is the **church of St. Paul-St. Louis★** (1627-41),
in the Jesuit style, rare in Paris. Madame de Sévigné used
to come here to listen to the preacher Bourdalone's ser-
mons. ▶ Coming from Rue St-Antoine, the N end of the
Marais is entered via the **Rue des Archives** *(to the right,
off Rue de Rivoli).* No. 22, next to the Lutheran Church,
is the medieval **Cloître des Billettes★** (cloister), built in
1415; the only construction of its kind to be seen in Paris.
▶ At the intersection with the Rue des Francs-Bourgeois
stands the **Hôtel Soubise★★** (1705-09), where the National Archives are housed around a fine **courtyard** in the
shape of a horseshoe. The superb apartments here
(decorated by Boffrand) are open to the public; these are
occupied by the **Museum of French History** *(2-5 daily
ex Tue.).*

▶ Behind this *hôtel* at No. 60 Rue des Archives, is the
Musée de la Chasse et de la Nature (Hunting Museum) in
the **Hôtel Guénégaud★,** 1650, recently restored *(10-5:30
daily ex Tue. and hols.)* ▶ **Rue des Francs-Bourgeois**
meets **Rue Vieille-du-Temple;** No. 87 of this street is the
Hôtel de Rohan★★, also a depository for national archives. No. 47, the **Hôtel des Ambassadeurs d'Hollande,**
dates from 1655; nearby, No. 31 Rue des Francs-Bourgeois is the **Hôtel d'Albret.** The proximity of these three
great houses demonstrates the heavy concentration of
aristocratic residences here during the 17thC. ▶ 14-16
Rue des Francs-Bourgeois is the **Hôtel Carnavalet★★** (→)
former home of Mme de Sévigné; this architectural masterpiece faces the **Hôtel de Lamoignon★★** (history library)
at 24 Rue Pavée... There are many others, too many to
enumerate, which mark the apogee of civil architecture in
France. A random choice might include the following : the
Hôtel Libéral-Bruant, Place Thorigny, now the **Bricart de
la Serrure** (Lock) **Museum;** the **Hôtel Salé★★,** nearby,
5 Rue de Thorigny, built in 1656 by the seigneur de Fontenay, is now the **Picasso Museum★★** (→) where in superb
surroundings the painter's personal collection is on display; the **Hôtel de Marle★,** 11 Rue Payenne.

▶ Rue des Francs-Bourgeois goes back to the **Place des
Vosges★★,** the heart and origin of the Marais. This is
where it all began : when Henri IV created this fascinating 127 m by 140 m square, he created a whole *quartier,*
almost a whole town. The buildings here are uniform in
design and the arcaded square is all but totally closed in
on itself. The white stone and red brick of the masonry,
tempered by dark blue slate roofing, give an impression
of purity and harmony. Victor Hugo lived at No. 6, the
Hôtel de Rohan-Guémenée, between 1833 and 1848 and
wrote some of his most famous works here. The house

is now a **museum** dedicated to the great author *(10-5:30; closed Mon. and Tue.)*, containing especially fine examples of his visionary and symbolist drawings.   □

▶ MEUDON

SNCF (Montparnasse station); R.E.R. line C. Bus: 136, 169, 179.

On the edge of its **forest** (wooded parks, play areas), at the foot of the terrace of its former château *(8:30-5:30 or 6;* view★★ of Paris) and its **Observatory,** Meudon is a residential town. **Historical museum** (11 Rue des Pierres) and **Rodin museum,** annex of the one in Paris, with the sculptor's tomb (19 Av. Rodin, *Sat. and Sun., 1:30-5).*   □

▶ Parc MONCEAU*

Map 4-B3 / 17th arr. Métro : Monceau. Bus : 30, 84, 94.

The Monceau Park is the last remnant of the immense domain belonging to the Orléans family, which at one time covered a large proportion of the land on the western side of Paris. During the Second Empire, when so many of Paris's parks and green spaces were created, the Parc Monceau was landscaped in the English style by the architect Alphand, providing verdant views for the luxurious houses built on its perimeter by notables and favourites of the régime.

▶ Well worth a visit are Nos. 5 and 7, Rue Murillo, and No. 5 **Avenue Van-Dyck.** ▶ Just off the park are two quiet and intimate museums housed in fine specimens of 19thC Paris mansions. At No. 7, **Avenue Vélasquez,** the **Cernuschi Museum★** was donated to the City of Paris by the great collector of Far Eastern art, Henri Cernuschi, in 1896 *(daily 10-5:40; closed Mon. and hols.)*. Considerably enlarged since then, notably with the addition of certain archaic pieces which are among the finest examples of their kind in the world. The upper floors contain objects ranging from the 2ndC BC to the 15th and 16thC AD. On the ground floor, courses in calligraphy and temporary exhibition. ▶ At 63, Rue de Monceau, the Camondo family's collection from the French 18thC is now in the possession of the Union des Arts Décoratifs (Decorative Arts Union). The **Nissim de Camondo Museum★** *(10-12 & 2-5; closed Mon., Tue. and hols.)* exhibits bronzes, porcelain objects, Savonnerie carpets, furniture (some from the royal household) and *boiseries.* The former salons are decorated with 23 Aubusson carpets★.   □

Unusual Museums :
Musée Baccarat

Also known as the Crystal Museum, this little establishment has been set up next to the salesrooms of the Baccarat company, Rue de Paradis (No. 30, 10th arr. 9-5; closed Sun.), in the street which is the commercial centre for the glass and porcelain industries. The Musée Baccarat offers a unique demonstration of the French glassworker's art, as practised by a company that has existed since the 18thC and has worked for all the great families of Europe, from the Romanovs to the Hapsburgs. On display are some of Baccarat's most beautiful creations : giant candelabras, flagons, bowls, beakers, and glasses, in every colour and style. This exhibition will make you view the other shop windows in the quartier with a decidedly jaundiced eye...

▶ MONTMARTRE**

Map 5-D3 / 18th arr. Métro : Blanche, Abbesses, Pigalle, Anvers, Lamarck-Caulaincourt. Bus : 67, 30, 54, 80, 85, 95. A minibus service serves the Butte Montmartre, from the Place Pigalle to the Mairie of the 18th arr., Rue Ordener ; funicular railway.

The Butte Montmartre has always been half dream and half reality, a mixture of the best and worst aspects of Paris. On the one hand, it is a mass of clichés and tourists ; on the other, if you know how to choose the time and place, it can lead you to delightful discoveries. This ambiguity is the source of its strange fascination.

▶ Nothing in Montmartres's long history ever indicated that it would become a great centre for bohemianism and the arts. The *Mont*, which was once dedicated to the God Mercury, is 130 metres high, one metre taller than the Buttes Chaumont and clearly dominating the Montagne Ste. Geneviève. During the reign of Charlemagne, it was named the "Mont des Martyrs", to commemorate the execution of St. Denis in AD 250. In 1133, a Benedictine abbey was founded here by Queen Adélaïde of Savoy ; the fields belonging to the abbey stretched out below, where the Grands Boulevards are now. Henri IV bombarded Paris from Montmartre's strategic heights ; later, mills began to appear, as the land grew more heavily cultivated. Montmartre pancakes and wine were consumed in *cabarets* or taverns. The Butte began to acquire a bad reputation ; libertine aristocrats built extravagant "follies" here, such as the Château des Brouillards, built by the Marquis de Pompignan in 1772. Then came the tragic events of 1815, when Montmartre put up a bloody resistance to the invading Cossacks. In 1871, hundreds of *Communard* rebels took refuge in the chalk mines of the Butte, where they were immured or blown up by the advancing Versaillais. To expiate their appalling massacre, the Third Republic erected the gigantic Basilica of Sacré-Cœur on the site. Even at this time, after Renoir and Van Gogh, unknown men of genius were beginning to converge on Montmartre from all over Europe : Van Dongen, Juan Gris, Picasso... the legend was born. At the beginning of 1914, Picasso was working on his *Demoiselles d'Avignon*, and Cubism had been founded. Montmartre and the Bateau-Lavoir entered history as the birthplace of modern art. ▶ Like a theatre backdrop, Montmartre has its "street" side and its "garden" side. The street side is mainly the **Boulevard de Clichy,** the **Place Blanche** and the vanes of the **Moulin Rouge** which go round and round all night. Then there is **Pigalle,** with its sex-shops and sordid striptease joints (now being replaced by peep-shows and video-clubs) ; its vaguely unsavoury fauna, and its overpriced bars and cabarets. ▶ Leaving the bright lights of "Gay Paree" behind, the **Rue Lepic** with its lively market★ leads through to the "garden" side of Montmartre. ▶ At No. 2, Rue Ronsard, in a former covered market is the **Museum d'Art Naïf** (Folk Art Museum), the Max Fourny collection of paintings and sculptures *(daily 10-6).* ▶ The climb to the famous **Moulin de la Galette★** is a steep one ; the latter was immortalized by Renoir and, is surrounded by houses from around 1900. Rue d'Orchampt leads down to the side of the Bateau-Lavoir at 5 Rue Ravignan, now demolished. ▶ On the other side of the Rue Lepic, **Avenue Junot** is surrounded by villas and gardens. ▶ In Rue des Saules, the **Lapin Agile Cabaret** still retains its rustic aspect ; it stands at the foot of the famous Montmartre vineyards, where the grapes are harvested every year amid all the trappings of country folklore. ▶ At No. 12, Rue Cortot near the **Rue Saint-Vincent** (Aristide Bruant had a song about this street), is the **Vieux-Montmartre Museum** *(2:30-5:30, 11-5 on Sun. ; closed Tue.),* possibly the only museum in the world exhibiting a completely reconstructed old-fashioned bistro. ▶ At the top of the long **Rue du Mont-Cenis,** which dips down in a northward direction towards Clignancourt, stands the **Basilica of Sacré-Cœur★** built according to plans by the architect Abadie, between 1876 and 1919. The Basilica makes up for its relative lack of architectural interest by providing a matchless view of Paris from its terraces — or, even better, from its dome. ▶ It is unfortunate that the Sacré-Cœur sometimes distracts attention from the lovely Romanesque Church of **Saint-Pierre-de-Montmartre★★**, the oldest sanctuary in Paris. There is doubt as to whether this structure embodies the remnant of a Gallo-Roman temple; however, its vaulted Gothic choir dates from 1147. A haven of coolness and peace, only a few steps away from the tourist frenzy of the **Place du Tertre★** with its cluttered café terraces, painters' easels and assembly-line artwork. ▶ The **Place du Calvaire** nearby is a veritable balcony over Paris, which can be both deserted and romantic at some hours. ▶ The steps, or the funicular, take you back down into the turmoil of the **Boulevard Rochechouart.**   ☐

Unusual museums : the Grevin waxworks

1982 was the centenary year of this museum of historical scenes and waxworks. A new ensemble devoted to 19thC Paris and its spectacles *(shows) has now been opened in Les Halles under the same auspices (10, Blvd. Montmartre, 9th arr. 1-7 daily, and Forum des Halles, level 1, 1st arr. 10:30-8 daily).*

▶ MONTPARNASSE

Map 9-C6 / 6th, 14th arrs. Métro : Montparnasse-Bienvenüe, Gaîté, Vavin. Bus : 28, 48, 58, 68, 82, 89, 91, 92, 94, 95, 96.

Montparnasse on the Left Bank, Montmartre on the Right. Their pasts are similar : dance-halls, rendez-vous for artists and exiles who became famous. Here their names are Modigliani, Matisse, Henry Miller, Hemingway, Lenin and Trotsky. Then there is the immense crowd that throngs the many cinemas on the Boulevard du Montparnasse and its periphery, and the terraces of the Dôme and Coupole restaurants (once the headquarters of the avant-garde). The same crowd overflows into the *crêperies* (pancake bars) of the Breton quarter, the Rue Delambre, the Rue de la Gaieté and the Montparnasse station precinct. The **Tour Maine-Montparnasse,** beside the triple-galleried **commercial centre,** in a sense matches the Sacré-Cœur; both are equally decried, but for good or ill their silhouettes are part of the Paris skyline. To the west, the **Bourdelle Museum★** (16 Rue Bourdelle, *10-5:30; closed Mon.*) is housed in a characteristic artist's building, a tangle of *ateliers* (studios) piled with scale models, sketches and plaster casts left by the sculptor. ▶ At No. 100, Rue d'Assas is the **Zadkine Museum★** *(10-5:40 daily ex Mon.),* in the house occupied by the sculptor between 1928 and his death in 1967. Three hundred of his works have been assembled in the building and its small garden, which were first opened to the public in 1982.   ☐

▶ The MOSQUE*

Map 11-E6 / Place du Puits-de-l'Ermite, 5th arr. Métro : Monge. Bus : 24, 47, 57, 61, 63, 67, 89.

▶ Built between 1922 and 1926 in the Moroccan style, the **Grand Mosque of Paris** *(10-12, 2-5:30; closed Fri. and Muslim holidays)* is decorated with considerable variety. The most diverse motifs in Islamic art have been used here, especially in the remarkable domed prayer hall. Many Parisians come to the *hammam* (baths) here, and greatly appreciate the cakes and mint tea available at the shops of the *souk*. Not far off are the **Arènes de Lutèce** (Rue Monge and Rue des Arènes), the heavily-restored remains of a Gallo-Roman amphitheatre which was destroyed in the 3rdC and rediscovered in the 19thC.   ☐

▶ La MUETTE and PASSY

Map p. 58-59 A2, 57-58 / 16th arr. Métro : La Muette, Passy. Bus : 22, 32, 52, 63, PC.

▶ The charming **Ranelagh Gardens** are laid out in the former park of a château lived in by Louis XV and Madame de Pompadour. The present château, hidden discreetly behind a screen of trees, was built at the beginning of the century by Baron de Rothschild. ▶ The resplendent **Marmottan Museum★★** (2 Rue Louis-Boilly, *10-6 ; closed Mon.*) is devoted to Impressionism ; one can see Monet's *Les Nymphéas,* which occupies an entire room. Monet's *Impression, soleil levant* was one of several stolen from the museum's collection. ▶ Discretion is also the hallmark of Balzac's house at No. 47, Rue Raynouard, where the writer used to come to escape his creditors. The resultant **Balzac Museum★** *(10-5:30 ; closed Tue.)* looks like a country house, with its garden. Balzac was not too happy here, finding it suffocatingly hot in summer and freezing cold in winter. While endeavouring to pursue his somewhat intricate pleasures, and nursing his love for the Polish Mme. Hanska from afar, Balzac nonetheless contrived to finish the last section of his great *Comédie Humaine* in this house. His spartan workroom has been left in its original state, complete with the famous coffee pot. The other rooms are stuffed with the memorabilia of a restless life : portraits, manuscripts, letters and everyday objects. ▶ The **Villa La Roche** (10 Sq. du Dr-Blanche), where the **Le Corbusier foundation** is located, illustrates the theories of the famous architect.   ☐

▶ NOTRE-DAME★★★

Map 11-E5 / 4th arr. Métro : Cité. Bus : 21, 24, 38, 47, 81, 85, 96.

World-famous masterpiece of the Middle Ages, perfect example of Gothic harmony. The Cathedral of Notre-Dame de Paris is more than a monument : it is a "history book", as Michelet has said. It should be visited at different hours of the day, for a full appreciation of the architecture of light embodied in the Gothic nave. Notre-Dame swarms perpetually with visitors, though it takes on a more authentic character during great religious ceremonies or organ recitals. The great organists of Europe come here to play the massive instrument installed in 1730 and rebuilt by Cavaillé-Coll during the 19thC *(free concert, Sun. pm).*

▶ The name of Maurice de Sully is closely associated with the construction of Notre-Dame ; after commencing the works, he directed them for thirty-three years until the completion of the choir and transept around 1200. Four more stages of construction had yet to be undertaken before France's largest cathedral was finally completed at the end of the 14thC. From that time onward, Notre-Dame has witnessed many great events : Saint-Louis' lying-in-state (1270) ; the solemn conversion of Henri IV (1594) ; the crowning of Napoléon I as Emperor (1804) ; the singing of the Victory Te Deum (1945) ; the funeral of General de Gaulle, attended by chiefs of state from all over the world (1970). Notre-Dame's historical importance is matched by its architecture as the symbol of Paris. All Gothic religious art was deeply influenced by it, to the farthest outposts of Europe. The architects Jean de Chelles and Pierre de Montreuil endowed their cathedral with simplicity and harmony, and proportions of 130 m long, 48 m wide and 35 m high from floor to roof. ▶ The **west façade,** enclosed by two massive square towers (69 m high) is divided into three levels : at the base stand the great doorways★★, with on the left a carved Virgin, in the centre the Last Judgment, and on the right, Saint Anne. This is surmounted by the Gallery of Kings (their heads have been replaced; some of the originals, knocked off by the Revolutionaries in 1793, are now in the Cluny Museum). Above them is the great rose window, 9.6 m in diameter, itself topped by an open gallery joining the two towers *(access to towers 10-4:30)*. ▶ The **lateral façades** and **the apse** have three levels backing on to each other; the apse itself is supported by flying buttresses with a span of 15 m. The 90-m spire was replaced by Viollet-le-Duc in 1860. ▶ The **interior** of Notre-Dame *(8-6:30 ex during services)* is composed of five naves, lit by three great rose windows★★ which still have their original 13thC stained glass. The side chapels contain 17th and 18thC paintings. ▶ The wooden choir stalls date from the 18thC; behind them is a magnificent screen decorated with a series of bas-reliefs★★ in polychrome stone. On the right, in the chancel, is the entrance to the Treasury, which displays gold plate, cameos of the various Popes, and a Palatine cross including a fragment of the True Cross. The **archaeological crypt** *(10-5)* displays objects discovered during the construction of the underground parking garage. ▶ Behind Notre-Dame, several parcels of the medieval street network disturbed by the Baron Haussmann are still visible. Rue Massillon, Nos. 4-8, fine 17th and 18thC homes; Rue Chanoinesse, Nos. 22 and 24, odd-looking canon's houses; finally, on the Rue de la Colombe, part of the Gallo-Roman defensive works built around the Île de la Cité.   □

▶ NOTRE-DAME-DE-LORETTE

Map 5-D3 / 16 Rue Chaptal, 9th arr. Métro : Saint-Georges, Blanche. Bus : 30, 54, 68, 67, 74, 85.

Behind the churches of **Notre-Dame-de-Lorette** (its forbidding exterior, not unlike a Greek temple, hides rich interior decoration) and the **Trinité** was a bustling neighbourhood of artists, painters, writers and musicians, which in the 19thC was referred to as "New Athens".

▶ Restoration and Second Empire buildings surround the Place Saint-Georges (Rues La Bruyère, de la Tour-des-Dames, d'Aumale, Ballu). ▶ The Orléans Square at No. 80, Rue Taitbout was the preferred spot for the love trysts of Chopin and George Sand in the 1840s; and their self-contained housing community was the home of A. Dumas, Delacroix and Heine. The community fall apart when the lovers separated, but the decor hasn't changed : the courtyards, gardens and neighbouring streets (like Rue Chaptal, where G. Sand, Chopin, Liszt and Renan visited the painter Ary Scheffer in his 1820 building) remain the same. The Scheffer home has become the **Renan-Scheffer Museum★**, a record of the intellectual and literary life of the 19thC and the New Athens *quartier* *(10-5:30, closed Mon.)*.   □

▶ OPÉRA**

Map 5-D4 / Place de l'Opéra, 9th arr. Métro : Chaussée d'Antin, Opéra. RER : Auber. Bus : 20, 21, 22, 27, 29, 42, 52, 53, 57, 66, 95.

Built at the behest of Napoleon III, the Paris Opéra boasts that it is the most important example of 19thC theatre architecture. Since the foundation of the Royal Academy of Music by Louis XIV, Paris had had nothing but temporary theatres, which were frequently destroyed by fire. The Second Empire bequeathed to Paris the great opera house it had always dreamed of, in the heart of Haussmann's new quarters.

▶ The original project for the Opéra was devised by Charles Garnier. It was opposed by the Empress Eugénie, who condemned the plans for their lack of style. The architect replied that they were "... in the style of Napoleon III, Madame." The period of construction lasted for 15 years, and incorporated a number of new construction techniques, especially the use of iron; work was interrupted by the Commune's insurrection and a series of financial difficulties. The building was finally inaugurated on 5 January 1875 by Marshal de Mac-Mahon; as of 1881, electric lights replaced the gaslights; and by 1964 Chagall's frescoes covered the ceiling of the opera house. Originally conceived for the social crowds of the Second Empire, the Opéra apportions more space to its public areas and salons than it does to the theatre itself. ▶ The sumptuous marble and onyx staircase★, the grand foyer★ with its mosaic-covered roof and the gigantic six-ton chandelier in the theatre bear witness to an omnipresent concern for display. This is particularly true of the ornate façade, with a replica of Carpeaux's famous sculpture group, *La Danse*. ▶ Lovers of opera and ballet will not overlook the little **Opéra Museum** *(10-5 daily ex Mon.)* in the West Pavilion, where designs, maquettes, decor and costumes recreate the magic of past productions mounted in the "Palais Garnier". □

▶ ORSAY Museum*

Map 10-C5 / Quai Anatole-France, 7th. arr. Métro : Solférino-Gare d'Orsay. RER : Gare d'Orsay. Bus : 24, 68, 69, 73, 84.

Inaugurated in December 1986, the Orsay Museum, built in the former Orsay station, presents works and documents tracing the evolution of the arts and French society from 1848 to 1914. The permanent collection is presented in the new galleries created by the Italian architectural designer Gae Aulenti, and includes paintings, sculptures and *objets d'art* from this period that were formerly displayed in the Louvre, Jeu de Paume Museum and the Palais de Tokyo *(10:30-6, Sun. 9-6, closed Mon.)*.

▶ **Painting :** all the Impressionist paintings once housed in the Jeu de Paume are here, representing a wide range from this period. ▶ **Sculpture :** under the high glassed roof, a vivid display from Carpeaux to Maillol. ▶ **Architecture and urbanisme :** scale models, drawings, reproductions *(East pavilions)*. ▶ **Art deco :** the eclectic tastes of the Second Empire and the tendencies of Art Nouveau are well-represented by furnishings by Hector Guimard, Horta, Majorelle, William Morris. ▶ Photography, graphic arts, publishing, cinema, books and posters are exhibited.   A sumptuous decor and an interesting view can be enjoyed at the **café des hauteurs.** □

▶ PALAIS OMNISPORT DE PARIS BERCY

Map 12-G7 / Quai de Bercy, 12th arr. Métro : Bercy. Bus : 24, 62.

Built over the former wine warehouses of Bercy, the elegant glass and metal construction (and practically vertical lawns!) of P.O.P.B. hide ingenious systems for adapting to athletic or artistic use; from Verdi to the "Six Jours" cycle race.

▶ The P.O.P.B. began the transformation of the Bercy *quartier,* which will continue with building renovation, a Finance Ministry and a 30-acre park. □

▶ PALAIS-ROYAL*

Map 10-D4 / 1st arr. Métro : Palais-Royal. Bus : 21, 27, 29, 39, 48, 67, 69, 72, 74, 81, 95.

The Palais-Royal is a marvelous, timeless enclave, set apart from the surrounding city, which seems to retain something of the 18thC which so loved it. Oddly, Parisians do not know it very well, though foreigners seem to be fully attuned to its charm. Built by Richelieu between 1629 and 1642, it was at first a "Palais-Cardinal", for it was here that Louis XIII's great minister lived and died. It became the Palais-Royal when the young Louis XIV moved in, with Anne of Austria.

▶ The regent Philippe of Orléans turned the Palace and **gardens★★** into a venue for his famous scandalous parties. After the destruction by fire of the Opéra close by, the Palace had to be reconstructed in 1763. The future Philippe-Égalité was so short of money to do this that he built **galleries** all round the gardens, which he rented to tradesmen, along with apartments in the upper stories. A second fire in 1781 destroyed the theatre on the site of today's **Comédie Française.** The Palais-Royal's bad reputation attracted crowds of common people; it was in the gardens that Camille Desmoulins called the populace to arms on 13 July 1789. Subsequently, the Palais Royal's gambling dens and cafés made it a haunt of men-about-town and dandies. Even Napoléon I, who installed the Council of State on the premises, failed to restore its former dignity. But fashion succeeded where authority had failed : the 19thC Paris crowd preferred the Grands Boulevards or the new *quartiers* to the Palais-Royal, and the gardens regained a tranquillity that has remained ever since. ▶ Behind the double portico of the Galerie d'Orléans, which separates the courtyard from the garden, the long galleries house a series of strange little shops selling military decorations, curios and lead soldiers. The main quadrangle is covered with a vast checkerboard by the artist Buren. Their rows correspond to the Palais-Royal colonnades. ▢

▶ The PANTHÉON*

Map 11-E6 / Place du Panthéon, 5th arr. Métro : Cardinal-Lemoine. RER : Luxembourg. Bus : 21, 24, 27, 38, 84, 85, 89.

The Republic has chosen coldness and austerity to an almost extreme to represent the virtues of its great men *(10-12 & 2-4).*

▶ The history of the Panthéon is hardly one of airy gaiety. Soufflot, the architect of what was then the church of Sainte-Geneviève, died of grief after seeing that his building was fissuring progressively as its dome was raised. The church had hardly been completed when it was turned into a Republican temple, by vote of the Constituent Assembly, in order to "receive the great men of the epoch of French liberty." Mirabeau was the first to enter it, followed by Voltaire, Rousseau and Marat. Some of the great men became less great after their Revolution : Mirabeau and Marat were forced to leave the premises, but the Third Republic installed Victor Hugo, Jean Jaurès and Gambetta. The day after his election, President François Mitterrand paid a visit to the building into which André Malraux had received the ashes of Jean Moulin, the Resistance hero, and where the frescoes of Puvis de Chavannes are in perfect harmony with the solemn, funereal atmosphere. ▢

▶ PASSAGES des GRANDS BOULEVARDS

Map 5-D4 / 2nd arr. Métro : Bourse, Richelieu-Drouot, Rue Montmartre. Bus : 20, 29, 31, 48, 67, 68, 74, 85.

On the margins of the congested Grands Boulevards (→), are 19thC galleries and covered arcades which offer highly interesting walks; they can be found all over, from the Palais-Royal to the Faubourg St. Denis. With their anachronistic decoration, daring metal-and-glass roofs, old-fashioned shops and tea salons, the "Passages" survive at one remove from the commercial mainstream. Some have been restored and given a new lease on life; others have become a trifle sordid and dilapidated. The oldest, such as the **Pas-**

sage des Panoramas★ (Blvd. Montmartre, opened in 1808), witnessed all the fashionable crowds of the Restoration; figures like Balzac and Chopin used to frequent their shops and restaurants.

▶ The most beautiful gallery in Paris is probably the **Galerie Vivienne★,** which is broad and airy, with monumental decor and elegant paving. Fashion boutiques and tea shops have given this *passage* new life. By contrast, the **Passage Véro-Dodat★** (1826), the **Passage Choiseul** and the **Passage Jouffroy** are devoted to old books, workshops or ... neglect. ▶ Not far from the Grands Boulevards, several galleries have opened in the Rue St-Denis. Most of these do a roaring trade. The **Passage du Caire** is a headquarters for the wholesale cloth trade. The **Passages du Grand Cerf** and **du Bourg-l'Abbé,** on the other hand, have contrived to preserve their original 19thC decor. Between the Rue du Faubourg-Saint-Denis and the Boulevard de Strasbourg, the **Passages Brady, du Désir, de l'Industrie** and **Reilhac** will soon be undergoing restoration of their statues and glassworks.   □

▶ PÈRE-LACHAISE Cemetery**

Map 13-H5 / 20th arr. Métro : Gambetta, Père-Lachaise. Bus : 26, 61, 69, 76.

The 125 acres of the Père-Lachaise Cemetery are half burial ground, half museum of 19thC sculpture. It is also a much-appreciated green area, full of tall trees *(7:30 or 8:30-5 or 6, according to season).*

▶ Opened in 1803 by the Municipality, Père-Lachaise is not unmarked by the publicity surrounding the legendary tomb of Héloïse and Abélard — but it has also had its authentically tragic moments. On 28 May 1871, the last 147 Communard insurgents were lined up and shot here against the **Mur des Fédérés** (Unionist's Wall); every year on the 1st of May, the procession of trade unionists comes to render them symbolic homage.   □

▶ PICASSO Museum**

Map 12-F5 / 5, Rue de Thorigny, 3rd arr. Métro : St-Sébastien-Froissard. Bus : 20, 29, 65, 96.

Inaugurated in September 1985, the Picasso Museum is housed in the Hôtel Salé, built in 1656 by Aubert de Fontenay, the collector of taxes on salt (hence the nickname "Salted Mansion"). The Classical-styled building, superbly restored, is in keeping with the painter's preference for old residences; 6 000 m² were cleared, and Diego Giacometti, the sculptor's brother, created the furniture and light fixtures *(daily 9:45-5:15 ex Tue).*

▶ This exceptional collection, comprised of 203 paintings, 158 sculptures, more than 3 000 drawings and prints, collages and ceramics, was assembled according to a French law which permits payment of inheritance taxes with art works. Furthermore, Jacqueline Picasso contributed the painter's personal collection (paintings and drawings by Renoir, Cézanne, Rousseau, Derain, Braque, Matisse, Miró). The whole, unique in the world, permits a vast overview of the work of one of the century's greatest artists.   □

▶ Musée de la PUBLICITÉ
  (Advertising Museum)

Map 6-E3 / 18, Rue de Paradis, 10th arr. Métro : Gare de l'Est, Château-d'Eau. Bus : 32, 39, 48.

This unique museum chronicles the precursors of the industry, along with its often neglected masters, whose talents have brightened the walls of city buildings over the years. Collection constantly being added to *(12-6 ex Tue.)*. Posters by Toulouse-Lautrec, Mucha, Erté, Jacno, Colin and Morvan; also fine protest work from 1968 and a mine of cinema and TV publicity footage. Finally, notice the building itself, formerly the store for the Faïenceries de Choisy-le-Roi; in the courtyard and interior, very fine ceramic panels.☐

▶ RODIN Museum**

Map 9-C5 / 77, Rue de Varenne, 7th arr. Métro : Varenne. Bus : 69, 87.

The splendid **Hôtel Biron,** built in 1730 to plans by the architect Gabriel, was originally lent to Rodin in exchange for a donation of his work and collections.

▶ The Rodin Museum is now installed in the surroundings where Rodin lived and worked between 1908 and his death in 1917. It is really a museum-cum-garden, offering a delightful open setting for the sculptor's creations. Here are represented all the phases of Rodin's development, from his youth (around 1875) to his evolution toward modern art in 1895, and his subsequent maturity, covering the years from 1900 onwards. Among the famous works in the museum are : *The Kiss*★★, an astonishing Balzac series, *The Thinker*★, maquettes for the *Bourgeois de Calais*★★, plasters and studies. The collections left by Rodin are of considerable interest : they include Monet *(Paysage de Belle-Isle),* Renoir, and two of Van Gogh's most celebrated canvases, *Le Père Tanguy*★★ and *The Harvesters*★★. Temporary exhibits *(10-5:30, 4:30 in winter; closed Tue.).*   ☐

▶ SAINT-CLOUD

SNCF (Saint-Lazare station). Bus : 52, 72, 144, 175. Terraced above Boulogne, Saint-Cloud has lost its château, but the **park**★★ remains, where joggers mix with strollers. Steep paths lead down to the spectacular Grande Cascade (view★).   ☐

▶ Basilica of SAINT-DENIS***

Métro : Saint-Denis-Basilique. SNCF : all lines from Paris-Nord, except Crépy-en-Valois. Bus : 153, 155, 156, 170, 177.

Formerly an abbey church, the Basilica of Saint-Denis is one of the earliest examples of Gothic Art. The 13thC nave and transept are attributed to Pierre de Montreuil. The **narthex** (1130-40) under the towers of the façade marks the first use of the Gothic pointed arch in a large building. Hence the Basilica of St.-Denis is a prelude to the extraordinary flowering of Gothic art in the centuries that followed, though it is visited more for its historical associations than for its architecture.

▶ Legend has it that Saint Denis, after his decapitation in 250, walked all the way up to the north of Paris, head in hands, to be buried there. Here an abbey was founded in 775, and was renowned for its **porches**★★, **choir-room**★★ and 12thC **crypt** built by Abbot Suger. Following the example of King Dagobert and Hugues Capet, the Kings of France adopted the habit of having themselves buried in the basilica, which at intervals for over a thousand years resounded with the cry "Le Roi est mort, vive le Roi!" ("The King is dead, long live the King!"). During the Revolution, the royal tombs were desecrated and the statues mutilated; the treasury, which was the richest in all Christendom, was sold or melted down. For better or worse, Louis XVIII restored the basilica, of which he proved to be the last occupant. Among the **tombs**★★★ which trace the evolution of funeral art from the Merovingian to the Renaissance eras, can be seen the burial place of Louis d'Orléans★ (16thC), the urn containing the heart of François I and his tomb created by Philibert de l'Orme, the marble tomb of Isabelle d'Aragon, Philippe III le Hardi's 1300 tomb, the monumental tomb of Dagobert in the choir (influenced by Italian art), the tombs of Henri II and Catherine de Médicis, and finally, the recumbent representations of Louis XII and Anne de Bretagne★, quite realistic *(10-4)*. ▶ In the former convent of Saint-Denis, Rue Franciade, is the **Art and History Museum of Saint-Denis★** which exhibits, alongside Paul Éluard mementos, interesting historical documents on working-class life in the 19thC *(10-5:30; 2-6:30 Sun.; closed Tue.)*. ▶ The famous Christofle factory has been turned into a **museum** tracing the history of the art of goldsmithing (112 Rue A.-Croizat, métro : Porte-de-Paris. *10-5:30, closed Sat. and Sun.*).   □

▶ Church of SAINT-EUSTACHE*

Map 11-E5 / Rue du Jour, 1st arr. Métro : Les Halles. RER : Châtelet-Les Halles. Bus : 67, 74, 85.

This formidable stone building (1532-1640) has dominated Les Halles' skyline since the demolition of the old market. Its architecture is remarkably unified (considering that the work continued for over a century), the best of Renaissance style combining with the most sophisticated Gothic techniques.

▶ Saint-Eustache is only a church, despite its cathedral proportions. It was altered by Colbert, the parish benefactor (whose imposing tomb★ stands in a chapel behind the choir), then renovated by Baltard in the 19thC (façade); but its main tradition is musical. Rameau is buried here; Berlioz created and performed his Te Deum (1855) at Saint-Eustache, and Liszt gave a recital of his "Messe de Gran". The organ has been heavily restored; today, with its 8 000 pipes and broad variety of tones, it is one of the largest instruments of its kind in Paris. ▶ In 1986, a 72-ton sculptured head was installed at the foot of the church by Henri de Miller.   □

▶ SAINT-GERMAIN-DES-PRÉS**

Map 10-D5 / 6th arr. Métro : Saint-Germain-des-Prés. Bus : 39, 48, 63, 70, 86, 87, 95, 96.

More than just a church, more than just a *quartier,* Saint-Germain-des-Prés is heavily associated with the 1950s, when it was a centre for artists and intellectuals. Boris Vian's trumpet-playing, Juliette Greco's songs, the existentialists and the jazz cellars of Saint-Germain made the area's name, along with its famous cafés (the "Flore" and the "Deux Magots") and the venerable Brasserie Lipp. Places are hard to come by in these establishments, especially at Lipp, which is intensely exclusive at lunch and dinner times.

▶ Amid the turmoil, the **church of Saint-Germain-des-Prés★★** stands behind its massive bell tower porch (12thC), which has recently been cleaned. This building, though it has frequently been restored and repaired, constitutes the most important vestige of what used to be the oldest and most brilliant abbey in Paris. Saint Germain himself, who was bishop of Paris, inspired King Clovis to build a basilica on the Left Bank of the Seine in the year 545. The abbey that soon grew up around it took the name of Saint-Germain, and the foundations of the present church were laid in about the year 1000. The Romanesque nave is balanced by the early Gothic traits of the choir; the large paintings by H. Flandrin hanging here are somewhat aggressively 19thC. ▶ On the Rue de l'Abbaye side is the tomb of King Casimir of Poland (17thC) and a statue of St. François-Xavier by G. Coustou. ▶ Also nearby, but seeming a hundred miles from the bustle of the **Blvd. Saint-Germain,** is the tiny **Place Fürstenberg★,** with the air of a backward provincial town square. Nothing here but a lamp post and four catalpas on a small round island in the middle of an 18thC street. A few art galleries : No. 6 was **Delacroix's studio** until his death in 1863 (museum, *9:45-5:15; closed Tue.*). That's all : yet, for many this little square on the former abbey courtyard is one of the most enchanting spots in all Paris. ☐

Markets and flea markets

Markets play a considerable role in the life of a Paris quarter. Two of the most interesting are the excellently restored Marché Saint-Quentin *(corner of Blvd. Magenta and Rue de Chabrol), and the* Marché du Faubourg Saint-Martin *(Rue Bouchardon). Both are covered markets, strongly characteristic of turn-of-the-century metal architecture. The open-air markets in Rue Lepic, Place Maubert, Rue Mouffetard, Rue de Buci, Blvd. Raspail (Métro Rennes) and Blvd. de la Muette are mostly for food. Place d'Aligre has a food market with a small flea market adjoining. The biggest flea market is on the northern edge of town, at the Porte de Clignancourt (Sat., Sun. and Mon.); alas, few bargains are to be had there nowadays, since "real" antique dealers have moved in, paying high prices for sales locations. More in line with the flea market tradition (and more chancy, perhaps) are the "Puces de Montreuil" (small furniture, curios and bric-à-brac), the "Puces de la Porte de Vanves", and the "Puces du Kremlin-Bicêtre", in the inner suburbs (Sat., Sun. am). Note also the secondhand bookstands along the Seine, the flower market on the Ile de la Cité, and the stamp market (Thur., Fri., Sat.) in the gardens off the Champs-Élysées.*

▶ Church of SAINT-JULIEN-LE-PAUVRE*

Map 11-E6 / Rue Saint-Julien-le-Pauvre, 5th arr. Métro : Maubert-Mutualité, Saint-Michel, Cité. RER : Saint-Michel. Bus : 21, 24, 27, 38, 47, 63, 85, 86, 87, 96.

The church of Saint-Julien-le-Pauvre has the air of a humble country church that has somehow wandered into one of the noisiest *quartiers* of Paris. The simplicity of this ancient sanctuary, which was once a shrine for pilgrims on their way to Santiago de Compostela, is a powerful contrast to the lavishness of the other great Parisian churches.

▶ Built in the 12thC, the church bears the scars of an eventful history. The style is halfway between Romanesque and Gothic; squat, without flying buttresses, St-Julien nestles in the shadows of its little **square**. Each year, concerts of ancient and modern music are held here, particularly during the Paris summer festival. Saint-Julien-le-Pauvre owes allegiance to the Graeco-Byzantine church (closely akin to Greek Orthodox). ▶ Nearby is another sanctuary of a different kind. On the Rue de la Bûcherie, *Shakespeare and Company* is the temple of Anglo-Saxon literature in Paris, where everyone who was anyone in the small world of letters, from Joyce to Hemingway, came to drink tea under the bookshelves. ☐

▶ Île SAINT-LOUIS**

Map 11-E5-6 / 4th arr. Métro : Cité, Hôtel-de-Ville, Pont-Marie. Bus : 24, 47, 67, 86, 87.

▶ Originally the Île Saint-Louis was two islands; they were joined together and developed just before the mid-17thC. The most beautiful houses date from this time

(Hôtel Chenizot★, 51 Rue St-Louis-en-l'Île : Hôtel Lauzun★, 17 Quai d'Anjou : Hôtel Lambert★, close by the Pont Sully). Nonetheless, it is the whole ensemble, rather than the individual buildings, which is important. Go down the **Quai d'Anjou**, the **Quai d'Orléans** (Nos. 6, 8, 20 and 22) and the **Quai de Bourbon**. With its glorious views★★ of the Cité, the Seine and the Left Bank, the Île Saint-Louis has managed to preserve its charm, in the face of the restaurants and *brasseries* which would wreck it, if they could. Unfortunately, the great houses here are defended with similar ferocity and, with the exception of the sumptuous Hôtel de Lauzun, they are almost impossible to visit. *(Visits to the latter are organized by the Centre d'Accueil de la Ville de Paris, 29 Rue de Rivoli.)*
▶ **Rue Saint-Louis-en-l'Île** is the best introduction to the island's special private atmosphere. No. 21, the **church of Saint-Louis★** (1656-1725) is in the Baroque Jesuit style. The chapels contain a fine selection of Italian paintings. But the street's most popular monument is unquestionably No. 31, which is Berthillon, the ice-cream shop ; one of the best in Paris. ☐

▶ Church of SAINT-MERRI

Map 11-E5 / 78, Rue Saint-Martin. 4th arr. Métro : Châtelet, Hôtel-de-Ville. Bus : 21, 38, 47, 58, 69, 70, 72, 74, 75, 76, 85, 96.

The first period of the Renaissance in France (1515-50) witnessed the building of a number of mansions between the Hôtel de Ville and the Rue Saint-Martin, which espoused the decorative principles of antiquity, as imported from Italy. Religious architecture, notwithstanding, remained faithful to the patterns set out during the golden age of Flamboyant Gothic ; and it was as a Gothic church that **Saint-Merri church** was planned. The 18thC to some extent bastardized it, with the copious addition of stucco and pompous motifs. This superimposed decoration has a certain advantage, all the same — looking at it, we may imagine what the vanished choir of Notre-Dame might have looked like. ☐

▶ Church of SAINT-SÉVERIN*

Map 11-E6 / Rue des Prêtres-Saint-Séverin. 5th arr. Metro : Saint-Michel. Bus : 21, 24, 27, 38, 47, 63, 81, 85, 86, 87, 96.

At the centre of this pedestrian precinct, with its medieval street-names (La Huchette, La Bûcherie, Le Chat-qui-Pêche) and pavement artists, the lovely **church of Saint-Séverin,** with its light and elegant nave, broods over the galleries of a 15thC charnel house (labeled a "cloister").

▶ Built between 1414 and 1520, then extended in 1670, Saint-Séverin boasts a singular marvel : the astonishing column in its ambulatory, which is a masterpiece of Flamboyant Gothic, with arches fanning out in the form of palm fronds from its summit. The technical perfection and complexity of this ensemble marks the watershed of several centuries of architectural development. Saint-Séverin's other claim to fame is its magnificent **organ** (used by composers Saint-Saëns and Fauré) with many parts dating from the 18thC. Frequent organ concerts are held here. Also, **stained glass★** (15th and 16thC) and modern windows by Bazaine. ☐

▶ SCEAUX

R.E.R. : line B. Bus : 128, 188, 194, 197, 297.

Colbert's château was destroyed, replaced by a replica which houses the **Ile-de-France Museum** (*9-12 & 4-6, closed Tue.* ; artistic and historical collections, exhibitions). The park, very "Grand Siècle", is intact ; see the Grand

Canal and the Octogone cascades, the Aurora pavilion (17thC), designed by Perrault, and the Hanover pavilion (18thC) which becomes a concert hall in summer.   □

▶ SÈVRES

Métro : Pont de Sèvres.

On the edge of the Saint-Cloud park, the **National Ceramics Museum★** retraces the history of this technique — and this art — from its origins to the present *(9:30-12 & 1:30-5, closed Tue.);* Islamic and Chinese pieces, works from Delft, Nevers and, of course, Sèvres.   □

▶ National TECHNIQUES Museum

Map 6-E4 / 270, Rue Saint-Martin, 3rd arr. Métro : Arts-et-Métiers, Temple. Bus : 20, 38, 39, 47, 75.

Founded by the 1794 Convention "to explain the construction and use of tools and machines", The **Arts and Trades Conservatory** was created for advanced technical education, but its museum *(1-5:30, 10-5:15 Sun.; closed Mon.)* is meant for the general public, which can discover the long and difficult history of the complex tools and machines now taken for granted.   □

▶ TUILERIES Gardens★★

Map 10-C4 / 1st arr. Métro : Concorde, Palais-Royal, Tuileries. Bus : 21, 24, 27, 39, 48, 68, 69, 72, 81, 95.

The Tuileries Gardens offer one of the most delightful walks in Paris, along the Seine, from the Louvre to the Concorde, a distance of about one kilometre. The terraces beside the river, the garden with its pools and fountains, the merry-go-rounds and children's playgrounds, cover a site where the grim palace of the Kings of France once stood, until it was burned down by the Communard insurgents in 1871.

▶ First, take a stroll round the **Carrousel Gardens,** past Napoléon I's small triumphal arch and the bronzes by Maillol; then walk the whole way along the terraces on the Seine side. ▶ At the top end of the Tuileries (Place de la Concorde) are the **Orangerie★★** *(9:45-5:15, closed Tue.)* and **Jeu de Paume Museums** *(closed for improvements; the collections have been transfered to the Orsay Museum).* Both date from the Second Empire. The Orangerie Museum, which contains *Les Nymphéas* (the Water-lilies) of Monet, has been transformed, and now holds the **Walter-Guillaume collection;** 144 masterpieces mostly of the 20s, by Soutine, Renoir, Cézanne and the Douanier Rousseau. It is a collection without parallel in France.   □

▶ Place VENDÔME★★

Map 5-C4 / 1st arr. Métro : Pyramides, Tuileries. Bus : 24, 42, 52, 84, 94.

Between the arcades of the Rue de Castiglione and the **Rue de la Paix,** the Place Vendôme opens out like a theatre set, starring the Ritz Hotel, Cartier, Van Cleef, Boucheron and others. This is the centre of the world of expensive jewelry and luxury products; the square itself is one of the most balanced and harmonious of the great squares built in honour of the Sun King, Louis XIV, an equestrian statue of whom once stood here — before the Revolution.

▶ Jules Hardouin-Mansart designed the Place Vendôme according to the requirements of Louvois and Louis XIV; the king and his minister were concerned for their future prestige, but they also had an eye for an excellent real-estate operation. The rigorous facades of the Place Vendôme, with their clear-cut horizontal lines, were completed in 1715 : the idea was that rich buyers could lay out their houses behind them just as they liked. Louis XIV's statue was knocked down during the Revolution, and replaced by Napoléon I with a tall column in his own honour. When the Bourbons returned after Waterloo, they appropriated this themselves by crowning it with their emblem, the *fleur-de-lys.* Louis-Philippe put back the statue of Napoléon I ; the Commune then pulled the whole thing down, at the instigation of the painter Courbet — and down it remained, for a few months. The unfortunate artist was sentenced to put it up again at his own expense ; the business ruined him, but it is to Courbet that we owe the present column and, at its top, the statue of Napoléon in Roman costume.   □

Art and antiques

The most prestigious antique dealers are located around the Quai Voltaire (B2 ; Métro : Bac), the Village Suisse *(A2 ; Ave. de Suffren ; Métro : La Motte-Picquet, closed Tue. and Wed.), and the Faubourg St. Honoré (No. 54, Antique Market ; closed Sun.). For Art Nouveau and Art Deco, Les Halles and the* Village St. Paul *(C3, Métro : Sully-Morland, 11-7 ; closed Tue. and Wed.), along with the plush* Louvre des Antiquaires *(11-7 ; closed Mon.) on the Place du Palais-Royal. Among the top art galleries,* Artcurial, *9, Ave. Matignon (B2 ; 11-7 ; closed Sun. and Mon.) is a kind of contemporary art supermarket, with something to suit every taste and (almost) every pocket. Not so its neighbours :* Bernheim-Jeune, *83, Rue du Faubourg Saint-Honoré ;* Maeght, *14, Rue de Téhéran ;* Marcel Bernheim, *35, Rue La Boétie ;* Wally Findlay, *2, Ave. Matignon. These galleries deal only in recognized — and expensive — artists. The Left Bank is more open to contemporary art :* Berggruen, *70, Rue de l'Université ;* Isy Brachot, *35, Rue Guénégaud ;* Claude Bernard, *9, Rue des Beaux-Arts ;* Stadler, *51, Rue de Seine. These establishments deal in modern trends ranging from hyperrealism to the new figurative art. Among the many small galleries in the Beaubourg quartier,* Daniel Templon, *30, Rue Beaubourg, stands out. For the experienced art lover, the best hunting ground is unquestionably the* Nouveau Drouot *auction rooms (9, Rue Drouot ; tel. (1) 42.46.17.11 ; 11-6 daily).*

▶ Place des VICTOIRES*

Map 5-D4 / 1st and 2nd arr. Métro : Bourse. Bus : 20, 21, 29, 39, 48, 67, 74, 85.

Designed like the Place Vendôme by Jules Hardouin-Mansart in honour of Louis XIV, the Place des Victoires was abandoned in the 19thC to merchants and tradesmen who installed shop windows in the beautiful 1700 facades.

▶ The Restoration replaced its equestrian statue of Louis XIV, but the whole spirit of the Place des Victoires was considered irretrievably lost when the Rue Étienne-Marcel was driven through in 1883. Fortunately, a concerted renovation project has now restored the Place to its former glory ; it has become a centre for high fashion and luxury ready-to-wear clothes. ▶ Nearby is the **church of Notre-Dame-des-Victoires,** founded by Louis XIII and built in the 17th and 18thC. More interesting, perhaps, than the bust of Lully (1702) or the fine *boiseries* in the choir, are the ex-voto tablets that cover the church's walls — there are more than 30 000 !   □

The canals

Once upon a time, one could float from La Villette to Meaux on a horse-drawn water coach... Those days are gone. All the same, the canals of Paris have mostly retained their curious setting, which made the unforgettable backdrop for Marcel Carné's great movie Hôtel du Nord. *The delightful Canal Saint-Martin gives the impression of being lost in Paris, as it wanders close by the roaring traffic of the Place de la République. The anachronistic pace of this waterway is regulated by the lazy barges churning slowly from lock to lock down to the Seine, behind the Ile Saint-Louis, under the Boulevard Richard-Lenoir and the Place de la Bastille and past the new marina in the Bassin de l'Arsenal. Napoléon 1st realized the great dream of Henri IV when he opened his network of canals through the heart of Paris. Nowadays, more than 10 000 barges pass along the various waterways every year, using the Canal Saint-Martin, the Canal de l'Ourcq or the Canal Saint-Denis; all three meet at the immense Bassin de la Villette, with its wharves, warehouses and workshops. Trip round the canals : embarkation La Patache (→ Practical information). Bus : Quai Anatole-France.*

▶ LA VILLETTE

Map p. 58-59 C1, 61 / 19th arr. Métro : Porte-de-Pantin, Porte-de-la-Villette. Bus : 75, 150, 151, 152, 251, PC.

The 140 acre park which occupies the site of the former slaughterhouses, constructed in 1866, of which survives the Mérindal★ Grande Halle (250 m long, 81 m wide, 25 m high), is the object of one of the greatest urban projects of our time. The largest attraction is the **Museum of Science, Technology and Industry** which houses permanent and temporary exhibitions, a planetarium *(Tue.-Sun., 2:30-7)*, a discovery centre for children, a media centre and a centre of education; the **"Géode"★**, a highly polished sphere of stainless steel, 36 m in diameter, containing a hemispherical spectacle-hall, equipped with a 1000 m² screen *(11-6:30, Tue., Thu., Sun.; 11 am-11:30 pm, Wed., Fri., Sat., closed Mon.)*; **Music City** comprises a conservatoire, an Instrument Museum, a centre of education and research and concert halls for both classical and modern music, of which the **"Zenith"** is already in operation. The park of 75 acres, crossed by the Ourcq Canal, will be enlivened by fountains, follies for games, restaurants and a centre for children.   □

▶ Forest and Château of VINCENNES

Map p. 58-59-C3 / Avenue de Paris, Vincennes. Métro : Château-de-Vincennes. Bus : 46, 56, 86.

The forest to which Saint Louis used to come to give judgement sitting under an oak-tree was cleared well before the Bois de Boulogne, at the beginning of the 18thC. The present facilities, lakes and rides of the **Bois de Vincennes** were organized during the Second Empire.

▶ The **zoological park★** *(9-5:30 or 6 in summer)* and **flower gardens** *(parc floral : 9:30-6:30)* attract many visitors from the eastern areas of Paris, as do the many grassy areas and sports grounds of the Bois de Vincennes.
▶ Not far from the flower gardens stand the forbidding walls of the **Château de Vincennes★**, surrounded by moats.   □

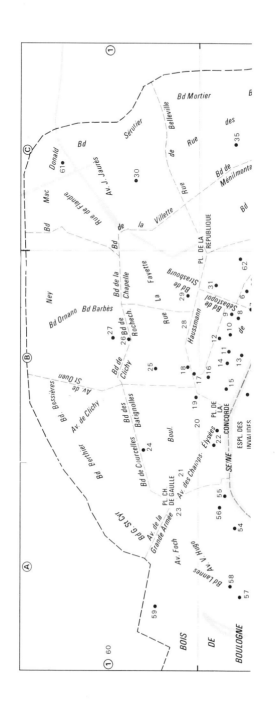

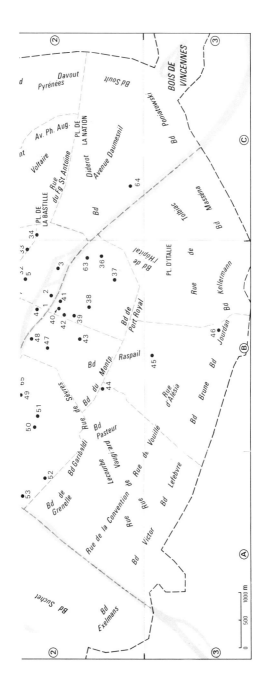

Practical information

Information : Paris : *Office de Tourisme de Paris,* 127, av. des Champs-Élysées, 75008, ☎ (1) 47.23.61.72. Open daily high season 9 am-10 pm (Sun 9 am-8 pm); low season, 9 am-8 pm (Sun 9 am-6 pm). Gare du Nord office : ☎ (1) 45.26.94.82, at the international train arrival area. Gare de l'Est office : arrival hall, ☎ (1) 46.07.17.73. Gare de Lyon office : "Grandes Lignes" exit area, ☎ (1) 44.43.33.24. Gare d'Austerlitz office : ☎ (1) 45.84.81.70, "Grandes Lignes" arrival area. Offices open daily ex Sun. Queues in summer can be long!

Maison d'information culturelle de la Ville de Paris : 26, rue Beaubourg, 75003. Open daily ex Sun. 10-8.

Bureau d'Accueil de la Ville de Paris, 29, rue de Rivoli, ☎ (1) 42.77.15.40 (ex Sun). **Hauts-de-Seine :** *C.D.T.,* 1, rue Trosy, 92140 Clamart, ☎ (1) 46.42.17.95. **Seine-Saint-Denis :** *C.D.T.,* 2, av. Gabriel-Péri, 93100 Montreuil, ☎ (1) 42.87.38.09. **Val-de-Marne :** *C.D.T.,* 11, av. de Nogent, 94130 Vincennes, ☎ (1) 48.08.13.00.

Entertainment : *Paris Informations Loisirs :* 24-hour service, ☎ (1) 47.20.94.94. In English : ☎ (1) 47.20.88.98. Deutsch : ☎ (1) 47.20.57.58.

Museums : *Paris Info-Musées,* ☎ (1) 42.78.73.81.

Embassies and consulates : *American Embassy,* 2, av. Gabriel, 75008, ☎ (1) 42.96.12.02, the Consulate is at 2, rue St-Florentin, 75008; *British Embassy,* 35, rue du Faubourg-St-Honoré, 75008, ☎ (1) 42.66.91.42, the Consulate is at 105-109; *Canadian Embassy,* 35, av. Montaigne, 75008, ☎ (1) 47.23.01.01 or (1) 47.23.52.20; *Irish Embassy,* 4, rue Rude, 75016, ☎ (1) 45.00.20.87.

S.O.S. : *SAMU* (emergency medical service) **Paris,** ☎ (1) 45.67.50.50. *S.O.S. Médecins,* ☎ (1) 47.07.77.77. *SAMU* **Hauts-de-Seine,** ☎ (1) 47.41.79.11. *SAMU* **Seine-Saint-Denis :** ☎ 17. *SAMU* **Val-de-Marne,** ☎ (1) 42.05.51.41. *Emergency poisoning centre,* ☎ (1) 42.05.63.29. *Police,* ☎ 17. *Lost and found,* 36, rue des Morillons, 75015, ☎ (1) 45.31.14.80.

Going out in Paris : the most detailed sources of information for the visitor are the weeklies *Une semaine de Paris-Pariscope, l'Officiel des Spectacles, 7 à Paris,* which come out on Wed and are sold at all newsstands; these weekly publications provide full information on theatres, shows, cinemas, concerts, exhibitions, festivals, etc., along with practical information and leisure centres. The *Kiosque de la Madeleine* (place de la Madeleine, from noon to 6), sells tickets half-price for same-day events. For restaurant information, ☎ (1) 43.59.12.12 or (1) 43.57.15.00 (Gault and Millau). The monthly English language newspaper *Passion* is also an excellent source of information on Parisian events and topics.

Guided tours : the C.N.M.H.S. (National Monuments Board; Monuments and Museums) organizes daily lectures and visits in Paris. Enq. : 62, rue Saint-Antoine, 75004, ☎ (1) 48.87.24.14, and in numerous daily newspapers. Independent lecturers and associations; see the forementioned weeklies and daily newspapers. *Cassettes Paris auto-guide* (self-guided tours on cassette), Paris T.O., Pompidou Centre, department stores, record stores.

Post Office : *Central Post Office,* 52, rue du Louvre, ☎ (1) 42.33.71.60. Open all night.

Banks : open daily ex Sat, Sun and nat hols. Some foreign exchange offices open on Sat. Banks close at noon on days preceding nat hols, and all day on nat hols.

✈   *Charles-de-Gaulle/Roissy-en-France,* 25 km N, ☎ (1) 48.62.22.80. *Air France :* information, ticket sales and reservations, ☎ (1) 45.35.61.61. *Air Inter :* information, reservations, ☎ (1) 45.39.25.25. Access : R.E.R. line B, direction *Roissy-Rail,* ☎ (1) 48.62.22.17, trains at approx 15 min intervals. R.A.T.P. bus n° 350 Gare de l'Est and Gare du Nord ; n° 351 departure pl. de la Nation, ☎ (1) 43.46.14.14. Air France buses ☎ (1) 48.64.30.20 : terminal at the corner of avenue Carnot, near the Arc de Triomphe.
Orly-Sud and *Ouest,* 14 km S, ☎ (1) 48.84.32.10. Access : R.E.R. line C, direction *Orly Rail,* ☎ (1) 48.84.38.60 ; trains at approx 15 min intervals until 9 pm. R.A.T.P. bus n° 215, ☎ (1) 43.46.14.14, departure pl. Denfert-Rochereau ; 183A, departure porte de Choisy, and 285, departure porte d'Italie, dir. Savigny-sur-Orge, which passes through the airport. Air France buses, ☎ (1) 43.23.97.10, Invalides terminal ; departure every 12 min.

S.N.C.F. (French Railways) Gare du Nord, northern region, ☎   (1) 42.80.03.03. Gare de l'Est, eastern region, ☎   (1) 42.08.49.90. Gare de Lyon, southeast region, ☎   (1) 43.45.92.22. Gare d'Austerlitz, southwest region, ☎   (1) 45.84.16.16. Gare Montparnasse, western region, ☎   (1) 45.38.52.29. Gare Saint-Lazare, western region, ☎ (1) 45.38.52.29. *Central enq. office :* ☎ (1) 45.82.50.50 or on Minitel : 3615 code SNCF. To make reservations at any station, ☎ (1) 45.65.60.60.

Métro : R.A.T.P. Central Enquiries Office : 53, quai des Grands-Augustins, 75006, ☎ (1) 43.46.14.14. Maps of the urban and regional express network are posted and distributed at all stations. The first trains run from 5 or 5:30 am for the regional express network (R.E.R.), and from 5:30 am for the urban metro. The last trains leave the terminus at between 12:30 and 1 am according to the line, all trains being scheduled to arrive at their final destinations by 1:15 am. Apart from the Charenton-Écoles — Créteil sections (line n° 8) and Carrefour Pleyel — St-Denis (line n° 13), cost of the Métro ticket (1st or 2nd class) is fixed, independent of the length of the journey or the number of changes of line.

R.E.R. : the Regional Express Network comprises three lines : Line A : Saint-Germain-en-Laye-Boissy-Saint-Léger or Marne-la-Vallée. Line B : Saint-Rémy-lès-Chevreuse or Robinson-Châtelet-Roissy or Mitry-Claye. Line C : Saint-Quentin-en-Yvelines-Dourdan, Massy or Étampes.

City bus service : the map of the city bus network is posted on Métro station quays, bus shelters and main bus stations. Except for the "PC" line (Petite Ceinture —.inner ring-road), the lines are numbered. Tariff : 1 2nd-class Métro ticket for 1 or 2 section trips, 2 Métro tickets for any trips exceeding 2 sections. Special tariffs for the PC line.
Tourist passes : these allow an unlimited number of trips for 2, 4 or 7 day periods on all R.A.T.P. lines (Métro, R.E.R., buses), and are sold in 50 Métro stations, in Paris ralway stations and at the Paris Tourism Office. If you are staying a while in Paris, it might be worth buying a *carte orange,* allowing unlimited travel for a 1 week calendar month on the R.A.T.P. networks, within the allocated zones ; or a *coupon jaune* valid (Mon-Sun). The R.A.T.P. also proposes *Formule 1* coupons, valid for one day.

Taxis : a few of the many taxi service numbers : ☎   (1) 47.39.33.33, (1) 42.03.99.99, (1) 42.05.77.77, (1) 42.70.41.41.

Driving in Paris : do not use your car in Paris unless it's absolutely necessary ; traffic is extremely dense, with numerous traffic jams. Parking places, if there are any, must be paid for. It is thus preferable to use public transport and to leave your vehicle at one of the many car-parks at the "portes de Paris" (the main entrances to the city on the ring-road, the Boulevard Périphérique).

Car-hire : *Avis,* 5, rue Bixio, 75007, ☎ (1) 45.50.32.31 ; 60, rue de Ponthieu, 75008, ☎ (1) 43.59.03.83 ; Gare St. Lazare, Quai No. 27, 75008, ☎ (1) 42.93.35.67 ; Gal. Élysées Rond-Point, 47, av. Franklin-Roosevelt, 75008, ☎ (1) 45.62.18.68 ; 184, rue du Fg-St-Martin, ☎ (1) 42.00.72.03 ; Gare de l'Est, 75010, ☎ (1) 42.00.72.03 ; Gare du Nord, Track No. 19, 75010, ☎ (1) 42.85.55.08/42.85.76.69 ; Gare de Lyon, 75012, ☎ (1) 43.42.10.41/43.43.14.52 ; 24, av. d'Ivry, 75013, ☎ (1) 45.83.21.93 ; Gare d'Austerlitz, Porte No. 25, 75013, ☎ (1) 45.84.22.10 ; 105, rue Lourmel, 75015, ☎ (1) 45.54.33.65 ; Gare de Montparnasse, Quai No. 19, 75015, ☎ (1) 43.21.62.12 ; 105, rue de Lourmel (with driver), ☎ (1) 45.54.33.65 ; 59, rue Pierre Demours, 75017, ☎ (1) 43.80.21.01 ; 8, bd Davout, ☎ 40.24.10.20 ; 78, av. Pierre Grenier, 92100 Boulogne-sur-Seine, 46.09.04.30 ; 99, av. Charles-de-Gaulle, 92200 Neuilly-sur-Seine, ☎ (1) 47.47.10.70. **At the airports :** Le Bourget, 1, av. du 8 mai 1945, ☎ (1) 48.38.51.00 ; Orly Ouest, ☎ (1) 48.84.44.91 ; aérogare de Roissy I, ☎ (1) 48.62.34.34 ; aérogare de Roissy II, ☎ (1) 48.62.59.59.

Aerial views of Paris : *Paris-Hélicoptère,* héliport de Paris, ☎ (1) 45.54.12.55 ; Métro Balard.

Paris by bus : *France Tourisme Paris Vision,* 214, rue de Rivoli, 75001, ☎ (1) 42.60.30.01 and 42.60.31.25. *Cityrama Rapid-Pullman,* 4, pl. des Pyramides, 75001, ☎ (1) 42.60.30.14.

Excursions on the Seine : *bateaux-mouches* (Seine pleasure boats) : pont de l'Alma, 75007, ☎ (1) 42.25.96.10. *Bateaux parisiens/Tour Eiffel,* pont d'Iéna, 75007, ☎ (1) 45.51.33.08. *Vedettes* (launches) du Pont-Neuf, pont Neuf, 75001, ☎ (1) 46.33.98.39. *Nautic Croisières,* quai du Point-du-Jour, pont de Boulogne, 92100 Boulogne, ☎ (1) 46.21.48.15. *Vedettes de Paris et de l'Ile-de-France,* pont de Suffren, 75007, ☎ (1) 47.05.71.29.

Bicycle rental : in many R.E.R. stations. *Le Bicy-club de France* organizes rambles and rents bicycles, info : 8, place de la Porte-de-Champerret, 75017 Paris, ☎ (1) 47.66.55.92. Bike paths, info : *Direction régionale de l'équipement,* 21, rue Miollis, 75032 Paris Cedex 15, ☎ (1) 45.67.55.03.

On the Paris canals : *Patache Eautobus,* a 3-hour morning excursion, leaving from the quai Anatole-France (Métro : Solférino) to the Villette basin, up the Seine and the Canal St-Martin ; vice versa in the afternoon, daily ex nat hols from May to Nov. Reservation essential : ☎ (1) 48.74.75.30. *Canauxrama :* from the Villette basin (Métro : Jean-Jaurès) to the Arsenal port (Métro : Bastille) ; the Canal de l'Ourcq, from Paris to Meaux. Reservations : 9 am-1 pm, ☎ (1) 46.24.86.16.

Markets : *Clignancourt flea-market,* avenue de la porte de Clignancourt, Sat, Sun and Mon, 7-7. *Flower-market :* Place des Ternes, 17th arr., daily ex Mon, 8-7 and at place de la Madeleine, 8th arr., same days and hours. *Bird market :* place Louis-Lépine, 4th arr., Sun. 9-7.

Auction rooms : *Nouveau Drouot,* 9, rue Drouot, 75009, ☎ (1) 42.46.17.11. Daily ex Sun, 11-6.

Cultural events : Apr-May : *Paris poetry festival,* place Saint-Sulpice ; *traditional arts festival.* **Jun :** *Mozart festival.* **Jul-Aug :** *festival du Marais ; festival estival de Paris ; festival de l'Orangerie de Sceaux.* **Sep-Dec :** *Paris chamber music festival.* **Oct :** *jazz festival.*

Other events : these are many and varied, including such events as the *Foire de Paris,* the *Salon du Prêt-à-Porter* and the *Paris Marathon.* Lists of these events can be found in the brochures published by the Paris Tourist Office and the Ville de Paris, and in the weeklies *Pariscope, L'Officiel des Spectacles,* etc.

Lodging for young people : *U.C.R.I.F.,* 20, rue J.-J.-Rousseau, 75001, ☎ (1) 42.36.88.18. *A.J.F.,* 12, rue des Barres, 75004, ☎ (1) 42.72.72.09.

Baby-sitting : *C.R.O.U.S.,* ☎ (1) 43.29.97.10 ; *Kid Service,* ☎ (1) 42.96.04.16.

Hotels-restaurants

✉ 75001

Hotels :
★★★★(L) *Intercontinental*, 3, rue de Castiglione,
☎ (1) 42.60.37.80, AE DC Euro Visa, 472 rm 27 apt ♨ ♋
ঌ 1650. Rest. ● ♦♦ *La Rôtisserie Rivoli* In summer, the
terrace blooms with flowers ; very nice food by J.-J. Bar-
bier and his kitchen brigade, 270-320♦ *Le Café Tuileries*
Discothèque *Estrela*. 150-210.
★★★★(L) *Jolly Hôtel Lotti*, 7, rue de Castiglione,
☎ (1) 42.60.37.34, Tx 240066, AE DC Euro Visa, 130 rm
♨ 1520. Rest. ♦♦ Grill as well, 210-320.
★★★★(L) *Meurice Inter-Continental*, 228, rue de Rivoli,
☎ (1) 42.60.38.60, Tx 230673, AE DC Euro Visa, 187 rm
♦ ♪ ♨ ঌ 1950. Rest. ♦♦♦♦ ♪ ♋ ✇ 200-380.
★★★★(L) *Ritz*, 15, pl. Vendôme, ☎ (1) 42.60.38.30,
Tx 220262, AE DC Euro Visa, 164 rm ⓟ ♦ ♨ ♋
♪ Favoured by Coco Chanel and Hemingway, 2460.
Rest. ● ♦♦♦♦ *L'Espadon* ♦ ♪ ✇ Even as we speak,
work continues on a huge underground site where a pool,
sports room and squash court, hair salon and late-night
bar are under construction. Rooms and suites, of course,
and the famous dining room where Guy Legay and his
staff pamper their faithful patrons : *brandade de morue
truffée, homard à la broche, steack "Coco Chanel", délice
glace Vendôme*. Prestigious cellar, 265-500 ; child : 230.
● ★★★★ *Saint-James et Albany*, 202, rue de Rivoli,
☎ (1) 42.60.31.60, Tx 213031, AE DC Euro Visa, 207 rm
3 apt ♨ ♋ ✇ 600. Rest. ♦♦ *Saint-James*, 140-300.
★★★★ *Cambon*, 3, rue Cambon, ☎ (1) 42.60.38.09,
Tx 240814, AE DC Euro Visa, 44 rm ⓟ ♋ 820.
★★★★ *Castille*, 37, rue Cambon, ☎ (1) 42.61.55.20,
Tx 213505, AE DC Euro Visa, 76 rm, 1080. Rest. ♦♦ *Le
Relais Castille* ঌ closed Sat and Sun , hols, 60-150.
★★★★ *Royal Saint-Honoré*, 13, rue d'Alger,
☎ 42.60.32.79, Tx 680429, AE DC Euro Visa, 80 rm ♦ 700.
Rest. ♦ ♪ ♋ closed Sat and Sun hols, 130-180.
★★★ *Les Halles*, (Novotel), pl. Marguerite-de-Navarre,
☎ (1) 42.21.31.31, Tx 216389, AE DC Euro Visa, 285 rm ♦
♋ ♪ ♨ ঌ 625. Rest. ♦♦ *La Rôtisserie* ♦ ♪ ঌ 130 ;
child : 45.
★★★ *Molière*, 21, rue Molière, ☎ (1) 42.96.22.01, AE DC
Euro Visa, 32 rm 3 apt ♋ 380.
● ★★ *Le Louvre*, 4, rue Croix-des-Petits-Champs,
☎ (1) 42.60.34.86, Tx 216405, AE DC Euro Visa, 56 rm ♨
ঌ A quiet street just a few steps from the Louvre, 370.
★★ *Agora*, 7, rue de la Cossonnerie, ☎ (1) 42.33.46.02,
Tx 260717, AE, 28 rm ⓟ ♦ ✇ 310.
★★ *Ducs de Bourgogne*, 19, rue du Pont-Neuf,
☎ (1) 42.33.95.64, Tx 216367, Euro Visa, 49 rm ♪ ✇ 290.

Restaurants :
● ♦♦♦♦ *Le Grand Véfour*, 17, rue de Beaujolais,
☎ (1) 42.96.56.27, AE DC Euro Visa, closed Sat noon and
Sun , Aug. Jean-Claude Lhonneur, formerly of *Le Céladon*, succeeds André Signoret who has left the *Véfour*
to replace Jean-Paul Bonin at the *Crillon*. And so it goes,
the waltz of the chefs in the Taittinger-owned restaurants.
Here, the great tradition of Raymond Oliver is scrupu-
lously respected : *oeufs Louis Oliver, sole Grand Véfour,
pot-au-feu de pigeon Gauthier, soufflé au chocolat*,
250-550.
● ♦♦♦ *Carré des Feuillants*, 14, rue de Castiglione,
☎ (1) 42.86.82.82, Visa ⓟ ঌ closed Sat and Sun. In
a pretty setting decorated by Slavik, Alain Dutournier and
his staff are really cooking. The *carte* is quite different
from the old *Trou Gascon* (now ably managed by Mme
Dutournier), but allusions to the chef's native Southwest

abound : *raviolis de foie gras à la truffe, croustade légère d'anguille à l'oseille et aux pruneaux, agneau de Pauillac rôti à la broche, pièce de bœuf de Bazas grillée au charbon de bois*. The cellar, Dutournier's pet passion, holds over 500 different great and modest vintages, 400-500.

● ♦♦♦ *Gérard Besson*, (I.L.A.), 5, rue du Coq-Héron, ☎ (1) 42.33.14.74, Visa ⌖ 💺 🐾 closed Sat noon and Sun, 3 wk in Jul, 2 at Xmas. Gérard Besson, a prize-winning pupil of the late, great Georges Garin, has just freshened up his quarters. The delicious food hasn't changed, we're glad to report : *ragoût d'huîtres, chipolatas et champignons à la crème de crevette*, game in season, 220-350.

● ♦♦♦ *Hubert*, 25, rue de Richelieu, ☎ (1) 42.96.08.47, AE DC Visa ♪ closed Mon noon and Sun. Hubert and his sweet spouse Joëlle have finally made their dream come true. In a handsome setting, he devotes all his energy to making his food-loving patrons happy : *galette de pommes Maxim's au saumon, sauce cressonnette, sole aux oranges, baron de lapin rôti aux fines de claires d'Isigny*, 250-350.

● ♦♦♦ *Le Poquelin*, 17, rue Molière, ☎ (1) 42.96.22.19, AE DC Visa ♪ 💺 closed Sat noon and Sun, 1-21 Sep. Loiseau, Perraudin and other great young chefs who got their start here with Claude Verger, would surely approve the new decor and Michel Guillaumins'cuisine : *rognons de veau à l'ail confit, daurade rôtie à la peau de canard*, 150-280.

● ♦♦♦ *Pierre Traiteur*, 10, rue de Richelieu, ☎ (1) 42.96.09.17, AE DC Euro Visa, closed Sat and Sun, Aug. Guy Nouyrigat is taking a well-deserved rest. His trusty staff is now directed by M. and Mme Dez, a couple of pros. Nothing has changed : *terrines*, roast rabbit, generous and delicious *bœuf ficelle*. Excellent wines from the Loire, 250-300.

● ♦♦♦ *Vert Galant*, 42, quai des Orfèvres, ☎ (1) 43.26.26.76, AE DC Euro Visa ℙ 💺 closed Sat. With a view of the Seine, a few steps away from the Courthouse. Arguing cases and courtroom emotions make a person hungry! Spec : *sole grillée, caneton rôti, andouillette de Saint-Pierre*. Prices are reasonable - if you've just won your suit, 200-290.

● ♦♦♦ *Le Mercure Galant*, 15, rue des Petits-Champs, ☎ (1) 42.97.53.85, closed Sat noon and Sun , hols. A spacious 19thC restaurant serving savoury cuisine : *champignons farcis aux escargots et basilic, fricassée de volaille*. Special fixed-price meal in the evening, 300.

♦♦♦ *Prunier-Madeleine*, 9, rue Duphot, ☎ (1) 42.60.36.04, AE DC Euro Visa 💺 💺 Wonderful seafood : *filet de turbot, filet boston*, 200-400.

● ♦♦ *Chez la Vieille*, 37, rue de l'Arbre-Sec, ☎ (1) 42.60.15.78, closed eves. Adrienne Biasin, the eponymous 'vieille' is now a media darling, but none of it has gone to her head - her restaurant has always enjoyed capacity crowds. The prices at her tiny bistro are just the same - don't forget to reserve if you want to sample the generous hors d'oeuvre and dessert buffets. *Rognons, foie de veau, pot-au-feu, plat de côte*, etc... A good place for a final blow-out before you start that diet, 250-300.

● ♦♦ *Chez Pauline*, 5, rue Villedo, ☎ (1) 42.96.20.70, Visa, closed Sat eve and Sun, 27 Jun-28 Jul, 24-31 Dec. André Génin brilliantly maintains the bistro quality of his father's hearty cuisine : Game in season, stuffed cabbage, *lapereau en gelée*. But in this new decor, he is inspired to add a few creations of his own : *queues de langoustines en bouillabaisse, salade de homard breton, pigeonneau rôti en croûte de sel*. All the Beaujolais *crus* are on hand, to quench your thirst, 300.

● ♦♦ *Le Globe d'Or*, 158, rue St-Honoré, ☎ (1) 42.60.23.37, AE Euro Visa ♪ closed Sat and Sun, Aug. Gérard Constiaux and his wife Christiane are sure to have food-lovers rushing to try their tasty, hearty Southwestern cookery : *jambon de pays grillé à l'échalote*, all kinds of duck dishes and good Madiran wine, 150-330.

● ♦♦ *A la Grille Saint-Honoré*, 15, pl. du Marché-St-Honoré, ☎ (1) 42.61.00.93, AE DC Visa ℙ 🎵 ♪ closed Sat and Sun. D. Cassagnes' savoury cuisine : *raviolis de crabe beurre blanc et herbes, filet de dorade grillé aux légumes frits, pot-au-feu "la Grille"*, 145-240.

● ◆◆ **Goumard**, 17, rue Duphot, ☎ (1) 42.60.36.07, AE DC Euro Visa, closed Sun. Lovely fish well prepared and tariffed at what the market will bear, 350.

● ◆◆ **Les Bouchôleurs**, 34, rue de Richelieu, ☎ (1) 42.96.06.86 ᕈ closed Sat noon and Sun, 15 Apr-15 May. Mussels direct from Aiguilllon-sur-mer make fresh and delicious *mouclades*, 130.

● ◆◆ **Pharamond**, 24, rue de la Grande-Truanderie, ☎ (1) 42.33.06.72, AE DC Visa ҉ closed Mon noon and Sun , Jul. Here's where to come for wonderful tripe and an authentic Belle-Epoque decor. Cider, *Poiré*, choice vintages, 150.

● ◆◆ **Véro-Dodat**, 19, galerie Véro-Dodat, ☎ 45.08.92.06, AE DC Visa ҈ ♪ closed Mon noon and Sun, Sep. An adorable little restaurant in a famous pedestrian gallery (the gates close at 10pm). As in bygone days, one must ring at the entrance, 75-180.

◆◆ **Caveau François Villon**, 64, rue de l'Arbre-Sec, ☎ (1) 42.36.10.92, Euro Visa ҉ ♪ ᕈ closed Mon, Sat noon, Sun, 15-31 Aug. Simple, savoury fare served in a handsome 15thC cellar : *coquilles Saint-Jacques fraîches à la vanille en gousse* (in season), *rognons de veau à l'effilochée d'endives*, 170-200.

◆◆ **L'Escargot Montorgueil**, 38, rue Montorgueil, ☎ (1) 42.36.83.51, AE DC Euro Visa ᕈ closed 8 days around Aug 15. Lovely interior. Six featured snail dishes, *turbot Montorgueil*, 250.

◆◆ **Righi Palais Royal**, 2, pl. du Palais-Royal, ☎ (1) 42.61.16.00, AE DC Euro Visa ҈ ♪ Luxurious decor; pretty girls and fashionable regulars come for the enjoyable, quality Italian food. Piano-bar, 180.

● ◆ **Porte du Bonheur**, 8, rue du Mont-Thabor, ☎ (1) 42.60.55.99, AE DC Visa, closed Sat noon and Sun eve. Charmaine's exquisite welcome and Félix Chong's delicate cuisine make for a memorable meal, or astounding banquet (order in advance) : *crevettes aux gousses d'ail et sel parfumé, agneau sauté à la sauce d'huîtres*, 55-150.

● ◆ **Saudade**, 34, rue des Bourdonnais, ☎ (1) 42.36.30.71, AE DC Visa ҈ ♪ closed Sun, 1 Aug-6 Sep, 23-27 Dec. Portugal in Paris : plaintive fado music and *bacalhau*, the traditional salt-cod specialty, 160.

◆ **Au Pied de Cochon**, 6, rue Coquillière, ☎ (1) 42.36.11.75, AE DC Visa ℗ ♪ A Venetian look prevails in this veritable institution that never closes, 200.

◆ **Carr's**, 18, rue Thérèse, ☎ (1) 42.96.04.29, AE DC Euro Visa ҈ ♪ ᕈ closed Sun eve. Conall Carr has followed his heart's desire and opened a restaurant. Galway Bay oysters, Irish stew. You'll never feel lonely here. Rare Irish whiskeys, 95-130 ; child : 60.

◆ **La Main à la Pâte**, 35, rue St-Honoré, ☎ (1) 45.08.85.73, AE DC Visa ♪ closed Sun. Pleasant Italian food, served till late at night. Spec : *carpaccio, jardinet des Quatre-Pâtes*, 80-180.

◆ **La Vigne**, 30, rue de l'Arbre-Sec, ☎ (1) 42.60.13.55, Visa ℗ ♪ A young woman cooks traditional favourites in this old market-district bistro : *œufs en meurette, andouillette et tête de veau*, 150-180.

PARIS II

✉ 75002

Hotels :

★★★★(L) **Westminster**, 13, rue de la Paix, ☎ (1) 42.61.57.46, Tx 680035, AE DC Euro Visa, 102 rm ℗ ♪ ᕙ 1350. Rest. ● ◆◆◆ **Le Céladon**, closed Sat and Sun, 2 Aug-2 Sep. The decor is still pale green, to harmonize with the 17thC porcelain, but the chef is new : Joël Boilleaut who is 30 years old and loaded with talent, trained by Robuchon and Kéréver. Wonderful food : *ravioles de tourteaux au basilic, millefeuille de saumon et d'épinards à la moëlle, filet d'agneau de Pauillac rôti à la coriandre et pâtes fraîches, gratin de fruits rouges et son sorbet*, 190-240.

● ★★★★ *Edouard VII*, 39, av. de l'Opéra, ☎ (1) 42.61.56.90, Tx 680217, AE DC Visa ♪ 760. Rest. ♦ ♪ ㅎ closed Sat and Sun, 220-350.
★★★ *Ascot Opéra*, 2, rue Monsigny, ☎ (1) 42.96.87.66, AE DC Euro Visa, 36 rm, 450.
★★★ *Favart*, 5, rue Marivaux, ☎ (1) 42.97.59.83, Tx 213126, 38 rm ⫯ ⚭ ♪ ㅎ 376. Rest. ♦ *New-Yorker* ♪ closed Mon eve, Sat noon, 100.
★★★ *François*, 3, bd Montmartre, ☎ (1) 42.33.51.53, Tx 211097, AE DC Euro Visa, 64 rm 11 apt ⚭ 600.
● ★★ *Timhotel La Bourse*, 3, rue de la Banque, ☎ (1) 42.61.53.90, Tx 214488, AE DC Euro Visa, 46 rm ⫯ The latest link in the chain, near the Grands Boulevards, 370.
★★ *Nouveau Monde*, 98, rue de Cléry, ☎ (1) 42.33.22.37, 48 rm, 200.

Restaurants :
● ♦♦♦ *Auberge Perraudin*, 164, rue Montmartre, ☎ (1) 42.36.71.09, AE DC Visa ♪ ㅎ closed Sun. Claude Perraudin is proud to announce that he soon will have a new decor. His generous, straightforward cooking will doubtless gain a brand-new crowd of patrons, but the regulars will remain for the fabulous *foie gras* (on sale to take out), kidneys, lobsters, etc...At the usual reasonable prices, 150-300 ; child : 50.
● ♦♦ *La Corbeille*, 154, rue Montmartre, ☎ (1) 42.61.30.87, AE Euro Visa ♪ ㅎ closed Sat noon (l.s.), Sun, New Year's Day, 15-22 Aug. Good food by gifted chef J.-P. Cario : *duo de poissons crus à l'aneth, raviolis de foie gras de canard aux morilles, noisettes de marcassin Saint-Hubert*, 150-280.
♦♦ *Coup de cœur*, 19, rue St-Augustin, ☎ (1) 47.03.45.70, AE DC Euro Visa ♪ ㅎ closed Sat noon and Sun. A sweetheart of a restaurant ; excellent value, but a bit more effort is needed in the kitchen, 115-170.
♦♦ *Drouant*, 18, rue Gaillon, ☎ (1) 47.42.56.61 This restaurant famed as site of the "Goncourts», has opened again, completely restored, with the artistry of James Baron (formerly of Cholet), 400-600.
♦♦ *Le Vaudeville*, 29, rue Vivienne, ☎ (1) 42.33.39.31, AE DC Visa Charming, old-fashioned brasserie serving a chic clientele, 105-140.
♦ *Dona Flor*, 10, rue Dussoubs, ☎ (1) 42.36.46.55, AE Visa, closed Mon. A favourite with the capital's Brazilian community, from 8pm to 2am, 150-200.
♦ *Hollywood Savoy*, 44, rue N.-D.-des-Victoires, ☎ (1) 42.36.16.73, closed Sat noon. Where the stockbrokers meet and greet over lunch ; at dinner, jazz and American cuisine, 80-120.
♦ *L'Amanguier*, 110, rue de Richelieu, ☎ (1) 42.96.37.79, AE DC Visa ♪ closed 1st May. Winter garden, patio. Good food, quick service, 130.
♦ *Pile ou Face*, 52 bis, rue N.-D.-des-Victoires, ☎ (1) 42.33.64.33 ♪ closed Sat and Sun , Aug. Snappy waiters, fashionable food, 250.

PARIS III

✉ 75003

Hotels :
● ★★★★ *Pavillon de la Reine*, 28, pl. des Vosges, ☎ (1) 42.77.96.40, Tx 216160, AE DC Euro Visa, 49 rm Ⓟ ⩘ ⚭ ♪ ㅎ An enchanting hotel, 850.
★★★ *Little Palace Hotel*, 4, rue Salomon-de-Caus, ☎ (1) 42.72.08.15, 59 rm ⚭ 250. Rest. ♦ 70-100.
★★ *Roubaix*, 6, rue Greneta, ☎ (1) 42.72.89.91, 53 rm, 210.
★ *Grand Hôtel des Arts et Métiers*, 4, rue Borda, ☎ (1) 48.87.73.89, 34 rm ⫯ ⚭ 125.

Restaurants :
● ♦♦ *Ambassade d'Auvergne*, 22, rue du Grenier-St-Lazare, ☎ (1) 42.72.31.22, Visa, closed Sun. Outstanding, hearty cuisine that takes you right to the heart of Auvergne : *charcuteries, saucisse fraîche, aligot, soupe aux choux*... and good Auvergnat wines. Service until 1am, 170.

◆◆ *La Guirlande de Julie*, 25, pl. des Vosges, ☎ (1) 48.87.94.07, AE Visa, closed Mon and Tue, Feb, 160-240.
● ◆ *L'Ami Louis*, 32, rue du Vertbois, ☎ (1) 48.87.77.48, closed Mon and Tue , Jul, Aug. The bill is as big as the servings, 120-260.

PARIS IV

✉ 75004

Hotels :
★★★ *Deux Iles*, 59, rue St-Louis-en-l'Ile, ☎ (1) 43.26.13.35, 17 rm, 485.
★★★ *Lutèce*, 65, rue St-Louis-en-l'Ile, ☎ (1) 43.26.23.52, 23 rm ⬳ 485.
★★★ *Saint-Merry*, 78, rue de la Verrerie, ☎ (1) 42.78.14.15, 12 rm Ⓟ ≲ A 17thC presbytery, 420.
★★ *Célestins*, 1, rue Charles-V, ☎ (1) 48.87.87.04, 15 rm, closed Aug, 300.
★★ *Place des Vosges*, 12, rue de Birague, ☎ (1) 42.72.60.46, AE DC Euro Visa, 16 rm ≲ ⊗ 230.

Restaurants :
● ◆◆◆ *L'Ambroisie*, 9, pl. des Vosges, ☎ (1) 42.78.51.45, closed Mon noon and Sun, 2 wks in Aug. Bernard Pacaud has fallen in love with the discreet, provincial charm of this handsome square. Patrons agree that his fine cooking is all the better for the change of scene : *mousse de poivron, effeuillé de raie aux choux, millefeuille de framboises*, 220-400.
● ◆◆ *Au Quai des Ormes*, 72, quai de l'Hôtel-de-Ville, ☎ (1) 42.74.72.22, Visa ≲ closed Sat and Sun, 1-26 Aug. A skip and a jump from the mayor's office, the Masraffs keep their many customers very happy : *dos de Saint-Pierre grillé, poêlée de langoustines aux artichauts, rognons de veau rôti*. Low-calorie dishes, 140-280.
● ◆◆ *Le Dômarais*, 53 bis, rue des Francs-Bourgeois, ☎ (1) 42.74.54.17, AE Euro Visa ≲ ♪ closed Mon noon, Sat noon, Sun, 2-28 Aug. The unusual decor is a 15thC chapel, with an 18thC dome. Young Patrice Bougerol has people talking about his enjoyable cuisine : *estouffade d'escargots à l'ail doux, saumon à la moelle de bœuf, symphonie de chocolats*, 120-180.
◆◆ *Au Franc Pinot*, 1, quai de Bourbon, ☎ (1) 43.29.46.98, DC Euro Visa ♪ closed Mon and Sun. No fewer than 24 wines can be tasted at the bar of this handsome 17thC edifice, accompanied by tempting gourmet snacks. Light and original cuisine can be had in the splendid vaulted cellar : *filet d'agneau rôti aux langoustines*, 130-250.
◆◆ *Bofinger*, 5, rue de la Bastille, ☎ (1) 42.72.87.82, AE DC Euro Visa ⬳ The oldest brasserie in Paris : seafood year round, *choucroutes*. Varied *à la carte* offerings and a fine selection of Alsatian wines, 140-150.
◆◆ *Chez Julien*, 1, rue du Pont-Louis-Philippe, ☎ (1) 42.78.31.64, AE Visa, closed Mon, Sat noon, Sun, 10 Aug-3 Sep, 250.
◆◆ *Coconnas*, 2 bis, pl. des Vosges, ☎ (1) 42.78.58.16, AE DC Euro Visa Ⓟ ≲ closed Mon and Tue, 15 Dec-15 Jan. Claude *(La Tour d'Argent)* Terrail's pet restaurant, 160-250.
◆◆ *Wally Saharien*, 16-18, rue Le Regrattier, ☎ (1) 43.25.01.39, DC Visa, closed lunch and Sun. The culinary subtleties of the desert are to be found here. All the wine you can drink, 230.
● ◆ *Le Monde des Chimères*, 69, rue St-Louis-en-l'Ile, ☎ (1) 43.54.45.27, Visa, closed Sun , Sep. The tradition continues ; a feminine touch in the kitchen and the dining-room, 100-150.

Send us your comments and suggestions; we will use them in the next edition.

♦ *Chez Benoît*, 20, rue St-Martin, ☎ (1) 42.72.25.76 Ⓟ closed Sat and Sun , Aug. Hearty food : *rosette du Beaujolais, compotier de bœuf en salade, boudin maison*, 350.
♦ *Jo Goldenberg*, 7, rue des Rosiers, ☎ (1) 48.87.20.16, DC Euro Visa ♪ The gathering spot of Paris's Jewish community : *zakouski*, pastrami, smoked salmon, 120.

PARIS V

✉ 75005

Hotels :
★★★ *Nations*, 54, rue Monge, ☎ (1) 43.26.45.24, Tx 205139, AE DC Euro Visa, 38 rm 🏡 Beflowered little patio, 400.
★★★ *Sélect Hôtel*, 1, pl. de la Sorbonne, ☎ (1) 46.34.14.80, Tx 201207, AE DC Visa, 69 rm Ⓟ ≼ ♪ 420.
● ★★ *Collège de France*, 7, rue Thénard, ☎ (1) 43.26.78.36, 29 rm, 320.
● ★★ *Grandes Ecoles*, 75, rue du Cardinal-Lemoine, ☎ (1) 43.26.79.23, 35 rm ≼ ▥ ⌬ Flower garden ; charming hotel near the Place de la Contrescarpe, 220.
★★ *Carmes*, 5, rue des Carmes, ☎ (1) 43.29.78.40, 38 rm ⅋ 250.
★★ *Esmeralda*, 4, rue St-Julien-le-Pauvre, ☎ (1) 43.54.19.20, Tx 270105, 19 rm ≼ ⌬ 270.
★★ *Trois Collèges*, 16, rue Cujas, ☎ (1) 43.54.67.30, Tx 206034, AE DC Euro Visa, 44 rm Ⓟ ≼ ⅋ 316.

Restaurants :
● ♦♦♦♦ *La Tour d'Argent*, 15-17, quai de la Tournelle, ☎ (1) 43.54.23.31, AE DC Visa Ⓟ ♿ closed Mon. For centuries, the *Tour d'Argent* has lived in close harmony with the Seine and Notre-Dame. Time cannot slow energetic Claude Terrail, the master of the tower, who trains his staff to honour the principles of perfect hospitality that his patrons have come to expect. Presiding over the pots (silver, naturally) in the kitchen is Dominique Bouchet, an exceptionally gifted young chef, who spent five years with Joël Robuchon : *persillé de homard en gelée aux aromates, petit homard froid Lagardère, marinière de rougets*. Nor are the classics forgotten : *foie gras des trois empereurs* and *le festival des canetons "Tour d'Argent", "Marco Polo", orange*, etc. Do visit the cellar and its memorable wine museum. Across the street, Tour d'Argent goodies are sold at the "Comptoir de la Tour", (tel. 46.33.45.58), 250-750.
● ♦♦♦ *Abélard*, 1, rue des Grands-Degrés, ☎ (1) 43.25.16.46, AE Euro Visa Ⓟ ≼ ▥ ⌬ ♪ closed Feb. Little by little, *Abélard* has made a place for itself, thanks to Patrick Pontoiseau's youthful style of cookery. The menu changes regularly, 100-200.
● ♦♦♦ *Dodin-Bouffant*, 25, rue Frédéric-Sauton, ☎ (1) 43.25.25.14, DC Visa, closed Sun , Aug. Dany and Maurice Cartier continue in Jacques Manière's tradition. Seawater tank for shellfish. Exemplary prices, 180-300.
● ♦♦♦ *Le Pactole*, 44, bd St-Germain, ☎ (1) 43.26.92.28, AE Euro Visa, closed Sat noon and Sun. The place is getting too small for all the diners who bid for a table. Roland Magne and his wife (who offers the smiling welcome, arranges flowers, pictures..) yearn for a new setting and new horizons. In the meantime, life goes on as does the fine cuisine that could benefit, we think, from a bit more diversity, 160-300.
● ♦♦ *Auberge de la Bûcherie*, 41, rue de la Bûcherie, ☎ (1) 43.54.78.06, AE DC Visa Ⓟ ≼ ♪ ♿ closed Mon noon. Cosy atmosphere with a fireplace and Lurçat tapestries, an appetizing menu and B. Bosque's refined cuisine : *langoustines au chou*, 280.
● ♦♦ *Clavel*, 65, quai de la Tournelle, ☎ (1) 46.33.18.65, Visa, closed Mon noon and Sun. All new, both management and decor. Outstanding food : *ravioles de homard, carré d'agneau rôti, pigeon farçi*, 160-300.

Be advised that hotels and restaurants in this Guide have perhaps changed addresses ; prices indicated are also subject to modifications.

● ♦♦ *La Truffière*, 4, rue Blainville, ☎ (1) 46.33.29.82, AE DC Euro Visa ♤ ♪ ᕼ closed Mon, 20 Jul-24 Aug. The Sainsard brothers perpetuate a solid culinary tradition : *foie gras, cassoulet, carré d'agneau farçi aux champignons*. Splendid Bordeaux vintages, 120-250.

● ♦♦ *Les Fêtes Gourmandes*, 17, rue de l'École-Polytechnique, ☎ (1) 43.26.10.40, Visa, closed Tue, 1-15 Jan. Let the feasting begin! Everyone's talking about young Vincent Gérard's affordably priced cuisine, 130.

● ♦♦ *Sud Ouest "L'Escarmouche"*, 40, rue de la Montagne-Ste-Geneviève, ☎ (1) 46.33.30.46, AE DC Euro Visa ♪ closed Sun, Aug. G. Bourgain's rich and generous cooking, served in a 13thC crypt : *magret, foie gras, cassoulets* (meat or fish), 200.

♦♦ *Auberge des Deux Signes*, 46, rue Galande, ☎ (1) 43.25.46.56, AE DC Euro Visa ≼ ♤ ♪ closed Sun. Historic decor, contemporary food : seafood, fish, 180-300.

♦♦ *Chez René*, 14, bd St-Germain, ☎ (1) 43.54.30.23, closed Sat and Sun, 26 Jul-3 Sep. Beaujolais wines and regional fare, 180-200.

● ♦ *Chez Toutoune*, 5, rue de Pontoise, ☎ (1) 43.26.56.81, Visa, closed Mon and Sun, 10 Aug-7 Sep, 24 Dec-2 Jan. An unbeatable fixed-price meal for 85F and a gourmet take-out shop (for pocket money?) next door, 85-110.

● ♦ *Restaurant "A"*, 5, rue de Poissy, ☎ (1) 46.33.85.54, AE Don't miss it : 18thC chinese cooking. Noble and traditional dishes, artistically carved vegetables that deserve to be displayed in a gourmet museum, 65-150.

● ♦ *Salut l'Artiste*, 22, rue Cujas, ☎ (1) 43.54.01.10, AE DC Euro Visa ♪ ᕼ closed Sun, Aug. Paul Chêne is understandably proud of his children and their nice little restaurant. Fair prices, 60-200.

● ♦ *Vivario*, 6, rue Cochin, ☎ (1) 43.25.08.19, closed Mon and Sun, 25 Dec-1 Jan. Good wines from the Corsican cooperative and specialties of similar origin make a great combination, 140-160.

♦ *Balzar*, 49, rue des Écoles, ☎ (1) 43.54.13.67, closed Tue, 1 Aug-2 Sep. A superb decor, great daily specials attract the scholars of the Collège de France and many Hachette employees : *foie de veau niçoise, bœuf gros sel, pieds de porc* and good beer, 140-185.

♦ *Bouquet du Port*, 4, bd de Port-Royal, ☎ (1) 47.07.08.99, AE DC Euro Visa ≼ ♪ ᕼ closed Mon, Tue noon, Sun eve, 8 Aug-8 Sep. Fish, oysters, seafood, 180-220.

♦ *L'Estrapade*, 15, rue de l'Estrapade, ☎ (1) 43.25.72.58, AE DC Euro Visa ≼ ♪ ᕼ closed Sat and Sun. Excellent seasonal fare at incredible prices. Limited space, 150.

PARIS VI

✉ 75006

Hotels :

● ★★★★(L) *Guy-Louis Duboucheron*, 13, rue des Beaux-Arts, ☎ (1) 43.25.27.22, Tx 270870, AE DC Euro Visa, 27 rm A most beautiful hotel, where O. Wilde stayed, 1700. Rest. ♦♦♦ closed Aug. Handsome bar. Well-conceived menu and fine cuisine, 220-310.

● ★★★★ *Relais Christine*, 3, rue Christine, ☎ (1) 43.26.71.80, Tx 202606, AE DC Euro Visa, 51 rm Ⓟ ▥ ♤ ♪ A superb hostelry in the heart of Saint-Germain-des-Prés, 1090.

★★★★ *Littré*, 9, rue Littré, ☎ (1) 45.44.38.68, Tx 203852, AE Euro Visa, 120 rm Ⓟ ♪ ⚘ 600. Rest. ♦♦ 125.

★★★★ *Lutétia-Concorde*, 43, bd Raspail, ☎ (1) 45.44.38.10, Tx 270424, AE DC Visa, 300 rm 17 apt Ⓟ ≼ ⚘ 800. Rest. ● ♦♦♦ *Le Paris* ♪ closed Mon and Sun , Aug. Jacky Fréon (Joël Robuchon's lieutenant at *les Célébrités*) and his staff wish you an excellent appetite in the stunningly decorated (Sonia Rykiel and Slavik) dining room : *piccatas de lotte, filet de canette nantaise, nougat glacé au coulis de framboise*, 220-340 ; child : 30.

★★★★ *Victoria Palace*, 6, rue Blaise-Desgoffe, ☎ (1) 45.44.38.16, Tx 270557, AE Euro Visa, 110 rm Ⓟ ⚘ 545. Rest. ♦♦ ᕼ ⚘ 120-160.

● ★★★ *Latitudes Saint-Germain*, 9, rue Saint-Benoît, ☎ 42.61.53.53, AE DC Euro Visa, 117 rm ⌕ ♪ A handsome job of renovation, providing every modern amenity, 720.

● ★★★ *Sainte-Beuve*, 9, rue Sainte-Beuve, ☎ 45.48.20.07, Tx 270182, 23 rm A small but comfortable and charming establishment, 650.

● ★★★ *Saints-Pères*, 65, rue des Saints-Pères, ☎ (1) 45.44.50.00, Tx 205424, Euro Visa, 40 rm ﷽ ⌕ 🛦 ꝑ ⌕ 500.

★★★ *Abbaye Saint-Germain*, 10, rue Cassette, ☎ (1) 45.44.38.11, 45 rm ﷽ ⌕ ꝑ 600.

★★★ *Madison Hôtel*, 143, bd Saint-Germain, ☎ (1) 43.29.72.50, Tx 201628, AE Visa 55 rm ⌕ 🛦 ꝑ ꝑ 700.

★★ *Balcons*, 3, rue Casimir-Delavigne, ☎ (1) 46.34.78.50, Euro Visa, 55 rm ⌕ ♪ 255.

★★ *Molière*, 14, rue de Vaugirard, ☎ (1) 46.34.18.80, AE Euro Visa, 15 rm, 250.

Restaurants :

● ◆◆◆ *Jacques Cagna*, (I.L.A.), 14, rue des Grands-Augustins, ☎ (1) 43.26.49.39, AE DC Euro Visa, closed Sat and Sun , Aug, 23 Dec-3 Jan. The most discreet of today's great young chefs will pamper you in his delightful and refined modern decor. Some of the dazzling possibilities : *pétoncles en coquille crémées au caviar, côte de bœuf "Angus", gâteau au chocolat et noix crème anglaise.* Great and simple wines. 195-500.

● ◆◆◆ *La Véranda*, 15, rue Princesse, ☎ (1) 43.26.90.22, AE DC Visa ⟆ closed Mon, Sat noon, Sun, 1-8 Feb, Jul. Way up atop the Club Princesse, Bernard Chirent, vice-president of the Troisgros alumni, cooks at the peak of his form (nothing less would do) for his demanding boss, Jean Castel, his friends and clients. Simple, very good food, 250.

● ◆◆◆ *Relais Louis XIII*, 8, rue des Grands-Augustins, ☎ (1) 43.26.75.96, AE DC Euro Visa ♪ closed Mon noon and Sun, 1-11 Jan, 3-31 Aug. Period atmosphere in this splendid old classified dwelling. Chef Martinez enlivens tradition with a youthful zest. The emphasis is on seafood : *assiette dégustation, rougets aux olives, millefeuilles de rognons.* Splendid cellar supervised by prize-winning sommelier, J. Chauché, 165-300.

● ◆◆ *Chez Dumonet*, 117, rue du Cherche-Midi, ☎ (1) 45.48.52.40, Visa, closed Sat and Sun, 30 Jun-1 Aug, 19-27 Dec. J. Dumonet, a seasonal sailor, cooks hearty straightforward dishes here in his handsome bistro, when he isn't out taming the seas. Exceptional cellar. Next door, charcoal-grilled specialties, 270.

● ◆◆ *Chez Gramond*, 5, rue de Fleurus, ☎ 42.22.28.89, closed Sun, 31 Jul-2 Sep. Where the Senate takes a lunch- or dinner-break : *escalopes de saumon sauce ciboulette*, 250.

● ◆◆ *Guy*, 6, rue Mabillon, ☎ (1) 43.54.87.61, Visa ♪ closed Mon noon and Sun, 10-20 Aug. There's a sweet samba in the air here : *feijoada, frigideira de langouste, rabada* and such pretty girls, especially at lunch on Saturday, 100-195.

● ◆◆ *Xavier Grégoire*, 80, rue du Cherche-Midi, ☎ (1) 45.44.72.72, AE Visa, closed Sat noon and Sun, 7-24 Aug. Xavier Grégoire's savoury cuisine is served in tiny, flower-filled dining rooms. Incredible fixed meal for 108 F. Spec : *filet de rouget au foie gras, escalope de saumon fumé*, 110-230.

● ◆◆ *Brasserie Lipp*, 151, bd St-Germain, ☎ (1) 45.48.53.91, closed Mon , Easter, Jul, 1 Nov, 22 Dec-5 Jan. Simply everyone comes here. You can't smoke a pipe but, illogically, cigars are acceptable, 160-220.

● ◆◆ *L'Apollinaire*, 168, bd St-Germain, ☎ (1) 43.26.50.30, AE DC Euro Visa ⌕ ♪ ꝑ closed 18 Dec-5 Jan. From the outside, it looks like a *brasserie*, but it is first-rate. Fine wines, 150-200.

Be advised that hotels and restaurants in this Guide have perhaps changed addresses; prices indicated are also subject to modifications.

● ◆◆ *La Foux*, 2, rue Clément, ☎ (1) 43.54.09.53, AE DC
♨ ♪ ♿ closed Sun, 1 Jan, 25 Dec. A publishers' hangout.
Big-hearted A. Guini, with an assist from his spouse,
maintains the Lyonnais traditions : *tablier de sapeur, foie
de veau des terreaux*. Real Lyonnais lunches on winter
Saturdays. The Brouilly flows freely. In summer, Niçois-
style snacks, 125-250.
● ◆◆ *La Petite Cour*, 8, rue Mabillon, ☎ (1) 43.26.52.26,
Euro Visa ⚜ ∰ ♨ closed Mon and Sun , open Mon eve in
summer, 20 Dec-5 Jan. Stéphane Oliver extends a smiling
welcome : *morue fraîche aux artichauts et pommes pail-
les, chartreuse de pigeon de Bresse*, 150-300.
● ◆◆ *Le   Caméléon*,   6,   rue   de   Chevreuse,
☎ (1) 43.20.63.43, closed Mon and Sun , Aug. Lots of
good humour and bonhomie here. Great food and delicious pastries. Nice wine list, 130.
● ◆◆ *Le Muniche and le Petit Zinc*, 25-27, rue de Buci,
☎ (1) 46.33.62.09, AE DC Euro Visa Quantity and quality.
Spacious dining room, booths, basement bar with a jazz
trio. *Choucroutes, foie gras, confits*, oyster bar. Take-out
shop open until 3am just a few steps away, 110-150.
◆◆ *Allard*, 41, rue St-André-des-Arts, ☎ (1) 43.26.48.23,
AE DC Euro Visa, closed Sat and Sun, 1 Jan, Aug, 25 Dec.
Mme Allard is gone, but the Burgundian tradition persists
in this well-known bistro, 280.
◆◆ *L'Echaudé St-Germain*, 21, rue de l'Echaudé,
☎ (1) 43.54.79.02, AE DC Euro Visa, 110-150.
◆◆ *La Closerie des Lilas*, 171, bd du Montparnasse,
☎ (1) 43.54.21.68, AE DC Euro Visa. Montparnasse
atmosphere, for a price, 230-500.
◆◆ *La   Grosse   Horloge*,   22,   rue   St-Benoît,
☎ (1) 42.22.22.63, AE DC Euro Visa. Time for fresh fish
and oysters all year round, 140.
◆◆ *Lapérouse*, 51, quai des Grands-Augustins,
☎ (1) 43.26.68.04, AE Euro Visa ⚜ 'We feed your passion',
say the ads. True enough, what with the delightful, romantic decor renovated by Pierre Pothier. But they aren't
nearly so good at feeding the patrons, 200-300.
◆◆ *La Vigneraie*, 16, rue du Dragon, ☎ 45.48.57.04, AE
DC Euro Visa ♪ closed Sun. Bruno Fava's outstanding cuisine raises this wine bar above the ordinary : *foie gras,
pot au feu, saumon à l'unilatéral*, 60-150.
◆◆ *Les   Arêtes*,   165,   bd   du   Montparnasse,
☎ (1) 43.26.23.98, closed Mon and Sat noon. Fresh from
the ocean, fish as you like it, 120-250.
● ◆ *Chez   Tante   Madée*,   11,   rue   Dupin,
☎ (1) 42.22.64.56, AE DC ♪ ♿ closed Sat noon and Sun.
Unusually affordable prices for truly enjoyable fare. Spec :
*ris de veau au coulis de langoustines et aux asper-
ges, canette fermière aux navets sautés et à la menthe*,
150-250.
● ◆ *Le Gourmet Gourmand*, 72, rue du Cherche-Midi,
☎ (1) 42.22.20.17, closed Mon and Sun, 19-26 Apr., Aug.
Excellent cuisine and the dynamism of J.-C. Adib, 200..
◆ *Drugstore Publicis Saint-Germain*, 149, bd St-Germain,
☎ (1) 42.22.92.50, AE DC Euro Visa, 50-70.
◆   *L'Epicerie   Landaise*,   10,   rue   Princesse,
☎ (1) 43.26.02.96, Euro Visa, closed Sun , hols and Aug.
The owner provides warm and generous Southwestern
dishes until 7am, 180-220.

PARIS VII

✉ 75007

Hotels :
★★★★(L) *Pont-Royal*, (Mapotel), 7, rue de Montalembert,
☎ (1) 45.44.38.27, Tx 270113, AE DC Euro Visa, 75 rm
5 apt Ⓟ ⚜ ♪ ♨ Library bar in the basement, 1100. Rest. ◆◆
Les Antiquaires ♪ ♿ closed Sun , Aug. Spec : *magret de
canard au confit d'oignon*, 150-200.
★★★★(L) *Sofitel-Paris-Invalides*, 32, rue St-Dominique,
☎ (1) 45.55.91.80, Tx 250019, AE DC Euro Visa, 112 rm
Ⓟ ♨ ♪ ♣ ♿ 1250. Rest. ● ◆◆ *Le Dauphin* ♪ ♿ Compe-
tently managed by Michel André Potier, this fine restaurant boasts light and inspired cuisine by Jacques Hébert
(a gifted Robuchon protégé), 200-350.
★★★★   *Montalembert*,   3,   rue   Montalembert,
☎ (1) 45.48.68.11, Tx 200132, Euro Visa, 61 rm ♿ 600.

● ★★★ *Saint-Simon*, 14, rue de Saint-Simon, ☎ (1) 45.48.35.66, 34 rm ⬭ ⬭ ⬭ 600.

★★★ *Cayré*, 4, bd Raspail, ☎ (1) 45.44.38.88, Tx 270577, AE DC Euro Visa, 130 rm [P] ⬭ 716.

★★★ *L'Académie*, 32, rue des Saints-Pères, ☎ (1) 45.48.36.22, Tx 205650, AE DC Euro Visa, 34 rm ♪ 440.

★★★ *Quai Voltaire*, 19, quai Voltaire, ☎ (1) 42.61.50.91, 33 rm ⟨ ⬭ ⬭ Exceptional view. Wilde and Wagner slept here, 350.

★★★ *Résidence Elysées-Maubourg* (I.L.A., Mapotel), 35, bd de Latour-Maubourg, ☎ (1) 45.56.10.78, Tx 206227, AE DC Euro Visa, 30 rm [P] ⬭ ⬭ ♪ Antique reproductions. Individual safes in the rooms, 500.

★★★ *Thoumieux*, 79, rue St-Dominique, ☎ (1) 47.05.49.75, Tx 205635, 10 rm ⬭ 375. Rest. ◆◆◆ ⬭ closed Mon. A neighbourhood institution, recently freshened up, 41-120.

★★★ *Université*, 22, rue de l'Université, ☎ (1) 42.61.09.39, 28 rm ⬭ ⬭ 450.

★★★ *Varenne*, 44, rue de Bourgogne, ☎ (1) 45.51.45.55, AE, 24 rm ⬭ ⬭ Two steps away from parliament, 350.

★★★ *Verneuil Saint-Germain*, 8, rue de Verneuil, ☎ (1) 42.60.24.16, Tx 205650, AE Euro Visa, 26 rm ⬭ ♪ 420.

● ★★ *Solférino*, 91, rue de Lille, ☎ (1) 47.05.85.54, Euro Visa, 33 rm ⬭ ⬭ closed 22 Dec-3 Jan, 340.

★★ *Lindbergh*, 5, rue Chomel, ☎ (1) 45.48.35.53, AE DC Euro Visa, 26 rm ⬭ ⬭ 320.

★★ *Résidence Latour-Maubourg*, 150, rue de Grenelle, ☎ (1) 45.51.75.28, 12 rm ⟨ ⬭ ⬭ A former private mansion, 300. Rest. ◆ ⬭ 68.

★★ *Vaneau*, 85, rue Vaneau, ☎ (1) 45.48.25.09, DC Euro Visa, 52 rm ⬭ 300.

Restaurants :

● ◆◆◆◆ *Jacques Le Divellec*, 107, rue de l'Université, ☎ (1) 45.51.91.96, AE DC Euro Visa ⬭ ⬭ closed Mon and Sun, 26 Jul-26 Aug, 23 Dec-3 Jan. Sporting fresh yacht-club colours, Jacques Le Divellec's restaurant near Les Invalides manages to bring the best of the sea to the city. Fresh fish, simply (beautifully) prepared : *rougets poêlés en laitue, dorade braisée au gamay, bar rôti à l'écaillé crème d'échalote*, 195-400.

● ◆◆◆◆ *Le Jules Verne*, Tower Eiffel, 2nd floor (elevator, south pillar), ☎ (1) 45.55.61.44, Tx 205789, AE Euro Visa [P] ⟨ ♪ ⬭ The world's most fabulous view, with an equally breathtaking decor by Slavik and wonderful food by Louis Grondard. Reservation necessary, 220-400.

● ◆◆◆◆ *Ravi*, 50, rue de Verneuil, ☎ (1) 42.61.17.28, AE DC Euro Visa [P] ♪ ⬭ Decor, service, table settings worthy of the greatest establishments. Ravi Gupta's entrancing Indian cuisine is absolutely first-rate. Fabulous tandoori curry, 105-300.

● ◆◆◆ *Arpège*, 84, rue de Varenne, ☎ (1) 45.51.20.02, AE DC Euro Visa ⬭ ♪ closed Sat noon and Sun, 1-17 Aug. On the site of Alain Senderens's former *Archestrate*, a talented young chef, Alain Passard, late of the *Duc d'Enghien*, has struck out on his own. Our nostalgia for bygone days quickly dissipates when we taste his light, personal style of cooking. Reasonable prices, 130-225.

● ◆◆◆ *Bistrot de Paris*, 33, rue de Lille, ☎ (1) 42.61.16.83, Euro Visa, closed Sat noon and Sun. A successful author and technical consultant to many important firms, Michel Oliver still finds time to manage his Bistrot, which for 20 years has played to capacity crowds. Excellent value here, witness the perfectly aged rib of beef and one of the least expensive wine lists in town, 200-300.

● ◆◆◆ *Duquesnoy la Bourgogne*, 6, av. Bosquet, ☎ (1) 47.05.96.78, AE DC Euro Visa [P] ⬭ closed Sat noon and Sun. A new start for the Duquesnoy couple, who leave the 5th arrondissement behind. Everything here is brand-new, from dining room to kitchen. Best of luck to them! *Terrine tiède de poireaux et langoustines, raviolis de homard et tourteaux, chartreuse de pigeon, feuillantine au citron*. Fine wines, 280-450.

● ◆◆◆ *La Cantine des Gourmets* (I.L.A.), 113, av. de La

Bourdonnais, ☎ (1) 47.05.47.96, AE DC Visa Ⓟ ♪ closed Mon and Sun. With surprising speed and maestria Régis Mahé, a close friend of super-chef Jacques Maximin, has conquered Paris with his refined, delicious cuisine. Attentive and smiling hostess Micheline Coat provides the perfect welcome and warm decor. *Soufflé d'artichaut au foie gras, pot-au-feu de pigeon, langue et rognon d'agneau, terrine aux trois chocolats*, 200-400.

● ♦♦♦ ***La Ferme Saint-Simon***, 6, rue de Saint-Simon, ☎ (1) 45.48.35.74, Euro Visa, closed Sat noon and Sun, 3-24 Aug. Thanks to his well-trained staffs, F. Vandehende successfully runs two Parisian eateries *(Le Manoir de Paris)*. Inspired, varied *carte*, fabulous pastries. Smiling Denise Fabre, a television personality (and Mme Vandehende) can often be seen supervising the dining room service, 150-270.

● ♦♦♦ ***Le Récamier***, 4, rue Récamier, ☎ (1) 42.22.51.75, DC Euro Visa closed Sun, 24-31 Dec. For politicians, publishers and plain old gourmets. You'd almost think you're in the country here in summer, at a table on the quiet terrace banked with flowers. Food is good, hearty and generously served. Owner Martin Cantegrit picks the best ingredients that the Rungis market has to offer : *œufs en meurette, fritures d'équilles, foie de veau*. The cellar holds some nicely-priced treasures, 300.

● ♦♦♦ ***Tan Dinh***, 60, rue de Verneuil, ☎ (1) 45.44.04.84, closed Sun, 1-15 Aug. In a brand-new and striking Asian setting, the Vifians serve their exciting Oriental specialties. The cellar is a veritable treasure trove. Take their advice when ordering wine : they are knowledgeable indeed, 300.

♦♦♦ ***Chez les Anges***, 54, bd de Latour-Maubourg, ☎ (1) 47.05.89.86, AE DC Euro Visa Ⓟ ♪ ♿ closed Mon and Sun eve. These angels are gourmets, 275-320.

● ♦♦ ***Chez Françoise***, aérogare des Invalides, ☎ (1) 47.05.49.03, AE DC Visa ♿ closed Mon and Sun eve , Aug. When the Assemblée takes a break, many of the members come here to refuel. Don't worry, regular folks are welcome too. Consistent quality : *foie gras frais maison, barbue grillée sauce vierge*, 100-170.

● ♦♦ ***La Boule d'Or***, 13, bd de Latour-Maubourg, ☎ (1) 47.05.50.18, closed Mon , Aug. Young Serge Barbey has got the ball rolling here with outstanding cuisine. His mentor, Bernard Loiseau, would surely approve. *Feuilleté de sole, symphonie de poissons marinés, pigeonneau rôti compote d'oignons, tarte fine Verger*, 170-300.

● ♦♦ ***Labrousse***, 4, rue Pierre-Leroux, ☎ (1) 43.06.99.39, AE Visa ♿ closed Sat noon and Sun, 1-21 Aug. After the luxury of the *Grand Véfour* where he presided in the kitchen, Yves Labrousse has opted for the almost provincial peace of a little side street to practice his culinary art : *œufs en meurette, feuilleté de rouget, pigeonneau en aumonière*, 125-270.

● ♦♦ ***La Flamberge***, 12, av. Rapp, ☎ (1) 47.05.91.37, AE DC Euro Visa, closed Sat noon and Sun. A great but modest chef at work here : *brochettes de Saint-Jacques au poivron doux*, game in season, *tarte chaude aux fruits*, 300-350.

● ♦♦ ***La Sologne***, 8, rue de Bellechasse, ☎ (1) 47.05.98.66, AE DC Visa Ⓟ ♿ The best selection of fresh game in season. Excellent Loire Valley wines. Next door at *Le Crik*, take-out foods and snacks, 100-210.

● ♦♦ ***Chez Gildo***, 153, rue de Grenelle, ☎ (1) 45.51.54.12, closed Mon and Sun Jul-Aug. Italian cuisine, 160-280.

● ♦♦ ***La Famiglia***, 34, rue de Bourgogne, ☎ (1) 45.55.80.75, AE DC Euro Visa. Pasta and more pasta... yes, but made by La Famiglia. They know what they're doing, Zoo.

● ♦♦ ***Le Perron***, 6, rue Perronet, ☎ (1) 45.44.71.51 closed Sun, 1-30 Aug. A little side street well known to lovers of pasta and good Sicilian cooking, 120-150.

● ♦♦ ***Vin sur Vin***, 20, rue de Montessuy, ☎ (1) 47.05.14.20, closed Sun. This friendly wine bar has become a full-fledged restaurant. Good food at affordable prices. Good wines, 150.

Send us your comments and suggestions; we will use them in the next edition.

♦♦ *Le Galant Verre*, 12, rue de Verneuil, ☎ (1) 42.60.84.56, AE DC Euro Visa ♨ ⑂ closed Sat noon and Sun, 225-260.

♦♦ *Relais Saint-Germain*, 190, bd St-Germain, ☎ (1) 42.22.21.35, Euro Visa. As ever, an excellent fixed-price meal, 80-170.

● ♦ *Au Pied de Fouet*, 45, rue de Babylone, ☎ (1) 47.05.12.27, closed Sat eve and Sun, 5-20 Apr, 2 Aug-6 Sep, 22 Dec-2 Jan. Hard to secure a table here, and hostess Andrée, by her own admission has something of a temper. Simple fare, but the homemade pastries are remarkable. Martial mans the bar, serving coffee and selected wines, 100-120.

● ♦ *Le Bellecour*, 22, rue Surcouf, ☎ 45.51.46.93, AE DC Euro Visa, closed Sat eve and Sun , Sat lunch, Oct-Jun, 10 Aug-1 Sep. Good Lyonnais fare, 200-250.

♦ *Aux Fins Gourmets*, 213, bd St-Germain, ☎ (1) 42.22.06.57, closed Sun, Aug. A good, inexpensive little place, 80-130.

♦ *Chez Germaine*, 30, rue Pierre-Leroux, ☎ (1) 42.73.28.34 ⌘ closed Sat eve and Sun, 28 Jul-1 Sep. Oil-cloth napery and simple, home-style fare, 40-70.

♦ *L'Oeillade*, 10, rue de Saint-Simon, ☎ (1) 42.22.01.60, AE DC Euro Visa, closed Sun. Good, inexpensive food with a feminine touch : *noix de coquilles Saint-Jacques, raie aux capres, magret d'oie au poivre*, 130.

♦ *La Belle France*, Eiffel Tower, 1st floor, ☎ (1) 45.55.20.04, Tx 205789, Euro Visa Ⓟ ⌇ ⌘ 80-180; child : 40.

PARIS VIII

✉ 75008

Hotels :

● ★★★★(L) *California*, 16, rue de Berri, ☎ (1) 43.59.93.00, Tx 660634, AE DC Euro Visa, 188 rm Ⓟ ⚶ ♨ ⚐ 995. Rest. ♦♦ closed Sun, 120-210.

● ★★★(L) *Claridge Bellman*, 37, rue François-ler, ☎ (1) 47.23.54.42, Tx 641150, AE DC Visa, 42 rm, 875. Rest. ♦♦ *Relais Bellman* ♪ ⑂ ⌘ closed Sat and Sun, Aug, 24 Dec-2 Jan. Handsome antique furniture, and a warm ambience rarely found in luxury hotels. Interesting food. Spec : *salade de crabe pamplemousse, suprême de barbue à l'angevine, cœur de filet à l'estragon*, 230.

★★★★(L) *Crillon*, (Concorde), 10, pl. de la Concorde, ☎ (1) 42.65.24.24, Tx 290204, AE DC Euro Visa, 189 rm Ⓟ ⌇ ⚶ ♪ ⑂ 1750. Rest. ● ♦♦♦ ♦♦ ⌇ ♪ ⌘ The fresh and lively decor devised by Sonia Rykiel contrasts picturesquely with the marble stateliness of Gabriel's 18thC palace. André Signoret, late of the *Grand Véfour*, returns to the *Crillon*'s kitchens : *Saint-Pierre aux poires et basilic, coeur de pigeonneau glacé de céleri, feuilles de chocolat aux épices*, 360-450. ♦♦ *L'Obélisque* Light fare from the grill, 120-210.

● ★★★★(L) *Le Bristol*, 112, rue du Fbg-Saint-Honoré, ☎ (1) 42.66.91.45, Tx 280961, AE DC Euro Visa, 200 rm Ⓟ ⚶ ♨ ⌘ ▣ Discreet luxury in a former 18thC cloister, 1800. Rest. ♦♦♦♦ ⌇ ⌘ Outstanding table, worthy of the hotel, 320-430.

● ★★★★(L) *Le Warwick*, 5, rue de Berri, ☎ (1) 45.63.14.11, Tx 642295, AE DC Euro Visa, 148 rm Ⓟ ⚶ ♨ ♪ 1650. Rest. ● ♦♦♦ *La Couronne* ♪ closed Sun eve , hols and Aug. Chef Bodiguel staunchly defends tradition : *ravioles d'écrevisses à la feuille d'estragon, fin ragoût de ris et rognons de veau*, 195.

★★★★(L) *Balzac*, 6, rue Balzac, ☎ (1) 45.61.97.22, Tx 290298, AE DC Euro Visa, 70 rm ⚶ 1400. Rest. ● ♦♦ *Le Sallambier* ♪ closed Sat and Sun. Pleasant decor, cuisine of Southwestern inspiration, prepared by a disciple of André Daguin. Nice selection of modest wines, 250-300.

★★★★(L) *George V*, 31, av. George-V, ☎ (1) 47.23.54.00, Tx 650082, AE DC Euro Visa, 288 rm ⚶ 2100. Rest. ♦♦♦ *Les Princes* ♪ closed hols. The surprising, flavourful cuisine of chef Pierre Larapidie is now featured here, in a luxurious setting, 220-400.

★★★★(L) *Lancaster*, 7, rue de Berri, ☎ (1) 43.59.90.43,

AE DC Euro Visa, 66 rm 10 apt ♿ 1600. Rest. ♦♦♦
closed Sat and Sun. Outstanding food, 160-300.
★★★★(L)   **Plaza-Athénée**,   25,   av.   Montaigne,
☎ (1) 47.23.78.33, Tx 650092, AE DC Euro Visa, 218 rm ≶
▥ ♪ ♿ 2000. Rest. ♦♦♦♦ Le Régence ♪ ♿ ⌗ 600.
★★★★(L) **Prince de Galles**, (Marriott), 33, av. George-V,
☎ (1) 47.23.55.11, Tx 280627, AE DC Euro Visa, 171 rm
♣ ♿ 1650. Rest. ● ♦♦♦ ≶ ♪ ⌗ Pierre-Dominique Cecil-
lon, sidekick of Joël Robuchon at the *Concorde* and the
Nikko, is shooting off sparks in his new kitchen : *petits
gris et grenouilles au pourpier, ravioles de loup au jus de
truffes, pied d'agneau farci, mousse vanille aux griottes*,
165-320 ; child : 100.
★★★★(L) **Pullman Windsor** (I.L.A.), 14, rue Beaujon,
☎ (1) 45.63.04.04, 135 rm, 950. Rest. ● ♦♦♦ Le Clovis,
closed Sat and Sun , Aug and hols. Chef Roue, a former
player on the Robuchon team, heads the side here in a
new decor : *tartare de dorade rose et saumon mariné,
grenouilles et écrevisses au sauternes, pigeonneau à la
feuille de vigne*, 125-300.
★★★★(L)   **Royal   Monceau**,   37,   av.   Hoche,
☎ (1) 45.61.98.00, Tx 650361, AE DC Euro Visa, 220 rm
▥ ◿ ⌗ ◲ 2140. Rest. ● ♦♦♦♦ Le Jardin ⌗ Light,
innovative cooking. Spec : *gourmandises de veau aux
aromates, suprême de volaille aux coquilles Saint-Jacques*, 240-400♦♦♦ Le Carpaccio ⌗ closed Aug. Italian
cuisine, 230-360.
● ★★★★   **Atala**,   10,   rue   Chateaubriand,
☎ (1) 45.62.01.62, Tx 640576, AE DC, 49 rm ▥ ◿ ♿ 650.
Rest. ♦♦ ♿ closed Sat and Sun , Aug, 180.
● ★★★★ **Résidence du Roy**, 8, rue François-1er,
☎ (1) 42.89.59.59, Tx 648452, AE DC Euro Visa, 36 rm Ⓟ
▥ ◿ ♿ 1300.
● ★★★★ **Résidence Maxim's**, 42, av. Gabriel,
☎ (1) 45.61.96.33, Tx 642794, AE DC Euro Visa, 4 rm
39 apt. Luxury and refinement : just don't ask the price.
Rest. ♦♦♦♦ Caviarteria The first link of an international
chain of prestigious hotels bearing the stamp of Pierre
Cardin : suites from 50 to 250 m², 2 bars, caviarteria,
health club and relaxation centre. So luxurious that price
simply isn't a consideration. Breakfast and tea served
under an arbour in a decor that resembles a painting by
Fragonard or Boucher. Maximum's bar open from noon
to 1am, 200-400.
★★★★   **Astor   l'Horset**,   11,   rue   d'Astorg,
☎ (1) 42.66.56.56, Tx 642737, AE DC Euro Visa, 128 rm
◿ ♪ 710. Rest. ♦♦ La Table de l'Astor, closed Sat and
Sun, 170-230.
★★★★ **Napoléon**, 40, av. de Friedland, ☎ (1) 47.66.02.02,
Tx 640609, AE DC Euro Visa, 140 rm, 1150. Rest. ♦♦
Baumann Napoléon ♪ Business specials, *saumon au vert,
saucisson froid de poissons à l'estragon, rognons de coq
en raviolis*, 215-300.
★★★★ **Royal Hôtel**, 33, av. Friedland, ☎ (1) 43.59.08.14,
Tx 280965, AE DC Euro Visa, 57 rm ≶ 723.
★★★★   **San   Régis**,   12,   rue   Jean-Goujon,
☎ (1) 43.59.41.90, Tx 643637, AE DC Visa, 44 rm ≶ ♪ En-
tirely renovated in 1986. Antique furniture, 1400. Rest. ♦♦
♪ ⌗ 190.
● ★★★ **Résidence Saint-Honoré**, 214, rue du Fbg-St-
Honoré, ☎ (1) 42.25.26.27, Tx 640524, AE DC Euro Visa,
91 rm ♪ ♣ 630.
★★★ **Franklin**, 19, rue Buffault, ☎ (1) 42.80.27.27, AE DC
Euro Visa, 64 rm ◿ ♿ 540. Rest. ♦ closed Sat and Sun ,
hols, 85-220.
★★   **Buckingham**,   45,   rue   des   Mathurins,
☎ (1) 42.65.81.62, AE DC Euro Visa, 35 rm ⌗ 360.
Rest. ♦ 70-200.
★★ **Ceramic Hôtel**, 34, av. de Wagram, ☎ (1) 42.27.20.30,
AE DC Euro Visa, 53 rm Astonishing façade covered with
ceramics, an Art-Deco hotel, 350.
★ **Bellevue**, 46, rue Pasquier, ☎ (1) 43.87.50.68, 48 rm
⌗ 140.

Restaurants :
● ♦♦♦♦   **Lamazère**,   23,   rue   de   Ponthieu,
☎ (1) 43.59.66.66, AE DC Euro Visa Ⓟ ◿ ♪ ⌗ closed
Sun , Jul, Aug, 31 Jul-1 Sep. The temple of truffles, *foie
gras*, and *confits* presided over by high priest and magi-
cian Roger Lamazère, 500-600.

● ◆◆◆◆ *Lasserre*, 17, av. Franklin-Roosevelt, ☎ (1) 43.59.53.43 ⌖ closed Mon noon and Sun, 2-31 Aug. Valiant René Lasserre deserves a special salute as a champion of classic French cuisine : *queues de langoustines rôties sauce sabayon, cassolette de ris de veau et crêtes de volailles au thym sauvage, nougat glacé aux fruits*, 400-600.

● ◆◆◆◆ *Le Bacchus Gourmand*, 21, rue François-1er, ☎ (1) 47.20.15.83, closed Sat and Sun. The new restaurant of the *Maison de la vigne et du vin*, is now a star in the gastronomic firmament thanks to the talents of Thierry Coué (a former colleague of Senderens at the latter's *Archestrate*), who gives full measure of his gifts in this plush setting. Flawless service. *Raviolis de pied d'agneau au safran, sole meunière aux oursins et oignons frits* (prepared tableside), *glace au miel*, pastries. Soon, a wine list representing the great French vintages, 250-450.

● ◆◆◆◆ *Le Pavillon Elysée*, 10, av. des Champs-Élysées, ☎ (1) 42.65.85.10, AE DC Visa Ⓟ ⌖ ⌖ closed Sat noon and Sun , Aug. A little shuffling of staff has taken place. Gaston Lenôtre remais in command, while young Didier Lanfray will henceforth preside in the kitchen preparing : *langoustines rôties sur jonchée de saumon, rougets à la fricassée de fenouil, canard rouennais , les mignardises* and chocolats, memorable pastries. *Les Jardins :* open every day all year round, with a 2-wk respite around Xmas, 300-450.

● ◆◆◆◆ *Lucas Carton (Alain Senderens)*, 9, pl. de la Madeleine, ☎ (1) 42.65.22.90, Tx 281088, Visa Ⓟ ⌖ ⌖ closed Sat and Sun, 1-23 Aug, 23 Dec-4 Jan. Hard by the Madeleine, a unique decor of blond paneling attributed to Majorelle (1859-1926). Eventhia oversees the flowers, the smiles, the welcome. Your tastebuds are catered to by Alain Senderens, explorer in the realm of French cuisine, who devotes an entire page of his menu to listing some 60 recipes he has created since 1968. Two other pages offer 6 *prix-fixe* meals (550-1000F, not incl. service), subtle harmonies of food and wines ; another page pairs wines and cheeses (18 varieties). To give you an idea : *raviolis de pétoncles, foie gras de canard aux choux à la vapeur, canard Apicius*. Old vintages. Private club upstairs, 550-1 000.

● ◆◆◆◆ *Taillevent*, 15, rue Lamennais, ☎ (1) 45.61.12.90 ♪ ⌖ closed Sat and Sun, 14-22 Feb, 25 Jul-24 Aug. The Duc de Morny would surely have enjoyed hosting the gourmet patrons who reserve far in advance to lunch or dine in his handsome town house. But J.-C. Vrinat does an impeccable job of it, assisted by chef Claude Deligne : *filet de sole artichauts et curry, noisettes d'agneau en chevreuil*. One of the world's best cellars, 530.

● ◆◆◆◆ *Maxim's*, 3, rue Royale, ☎ (1) 42.65.27.94, AE DC Euro Visa ⌖ closed Sun. Pierre Cardin sets the tone, chef Menant and his brigade do their best to follow : it's starting to jell. Upstairs, dinners and late suppers. Close by, *Minim's* and its (far) lower prices, 165-700.

◆◆◆◆ *Laurent*, 41, av. Gabriel, ☎ (1) 42.25.00.39, AE DC Ⓟ ♨ ♨ ♪ ⌖ ⌖ closed Sat noon and Sun. The pearl of the Golden Triangle of restaurants on the Champs-Élysées. Lobster salad, *langouste tiède en salade, canard nantais aux deux cuissons, soufflés Laurent*, 320-610.

◆◆◆◆ *Ledoyen*, (I.L.A.), Carré des Champs-Élysées, ☎ (1) 42.66.54.77 Ⓟ ⌖ ♨ ♨ ♪ ⌖ closed Sun , Aug. Under new management. Wait and see, 300-500.

● ◆◆◆ *Alain Rayé*, 49, rue du Colisée, ☎ (1) 42.25.66.76, DC Euro Visa ♨ ⌖ closed Sat noon and Sun. Alain Rayé, late of Albertville, serves outstanding cuisine at very Parisian prices, 165-290.

● ◆◆◆ *Chiberta*, 3, rue A.-Houssaye, ☎ (1) 45.63.77.90, closed Sat and Sun , hols and Aug. Louis-Noël Richard has many faithful clients whom he welcomes with flawless hospitality in his handsome establishment (the sober decor is by Jean Dives). The cuisine of impish, discreet Jean-Michel Bedier keeps all these customers satisfied, 350-420.

● ◆◆◆ *La Fermette Marbeuf 1900*, 5, rue Marbeuf, ☎ (1) 47.23.31.31, AE DC Visa ♪ Pleasant interior with a turn-of-the-century decor. Capable, sly Jean Laurent, his chef Gilbert Isaac and their dependable staff never cease to amaze us with their attention to detail. New menu : cheese tray, vintage wine list, cigars, smiles etc..., 125-190.

● ◆◆◆ *La Marée*, 1, rue Daru, ☎ (1) 47.63.52.42, AE DC Ⓟ closed Aug. The quality here is as regular as the tides that the restaurant is named for. Eric Trompier, the young owner-director has infused an agreeably youthful feel here, much to the patrons' approval (Mama quietly keeps an eye on things too). In the kitchen, Gérard Rouillard and his expert brigade send forth splendidly simple fish and seafood dishes : *belons au champagne, loup Marie-Do, turbotin, rougets grillés, farandole gourmande du chef pâtissier*. For the regulars, a few meat dishes. More than 600 wines on hand in the cellar, with the spotlight on Bordeaux in all price ranges, 250-400.

● ◆◆◆ *Le Bonaventure*, 35, rue Jean-Goujon, ☎ (1) 42.25.02.58, AE Visa ♪ closed Sat noon and Sun. An unobstrusive eatery in a quiet spot near the Alma. The little inner courtyard holds tables in fine weather. Noël Gutrin prepares some interesting dishes : *saumon à la tahitienne, poêlée de langoustines et Saint-Jacques aux cèpes, fricassée de ris et de rognons de veau au vinaigre de framboise*, 250.

● ◆◆◆ *Le Lord Gourmand*, 9, rue Lord-Byron, ☎ (1) 43.59.07.27, AE Euro Visa, closed Sat and Sun , Aug, 24-31 Dec. Model student Daniel Météry has caught up with his teachers (Bocuse, Troisgros). He pays them homage every day with his dazzling cuisine : *roulade de Saint-Jacques* (in season), *magret fumé, souris d'agneau aux pâtes fraîches, tarte tiède aux pommes et abricots*. Ask Brigitte for a cocktail, 160-300.

● ◆◆◆ *Fouquet's*, 99, av. des Champs-Élysées, ☎ (1) 47.23.70.60, AE DC Euro Visa ⸙ ঠ closed Sat and Sun , for *Fouquet's Élysées*, 18 Jul-23 Aug. The denizens of the theatre and film world come for the warm welcome of Maurice Casanova, for his daughter, Jenny Paule's charming smile and for P. Ducroux's good cooking. On the terrace, Paris and the Champs-Élysées are at your feet, 200-240.

◆◆◆ *Francis*, 7, pl. de l'Alma, ☎ (1) 47.20.86.83 Fish are the favoured food in this handsome, classy *brasserie*, 250.

● ◆◆ *Al Amir*, 66, rue François-1er, ☎ (1) 47.23.79.05, AE DC Visa ♪ ⧉ The charm of the East and the Arabian nights, just off the Champs-Élysées. Wonderful hot and cold *mezzes*, charcoal-grilled dishes and Le banese wines, 165-250.

● ◆◆ *Au Petit Montmorency*, 5, rue Rabelais, ☎ (1) 42.25.11.19, Euro Visa ⧉ closed Sun , Aug. In a quiet, propitiously named street, D. Bouché cooks up a stunning array of delicate flavours : *foie gras de canard au caramel poivré, canard Lucifer à la semoule, soufflé au chocolat*, 280.

● ◆◆ *Chez Edgard*, 4, rue Marbeuf, ☎ (1) 47.20.51.15, AE DC Euro Visa, closed Sun. A favourite with politicians, stars and radio personalities. Reserve, 230.

● ◆◆ *Jean-Charles et Ses Amis*, 7,rue de la Trémoille, ☎ (1) 47.23.88.18, closed Sat noon. Jean-Charles Diehl has lots of friends who appreciate his warm welcome and the cooking of chef J.-C. Billebault, 150-250.

● ◆◆ *Le Grenadin*, 46, rue de Naples, ☎ (1) 45.63.28.92, AE Euro Visa ♪ closed Sat and Sun , 3 wks in Aug, 23 Dec-2 Jan. Young Patrick Cirotte is a chef with a future : *émincé de rable de lapin à la crème d'ail, marinade de blanc de volaille*. His restaurant now holds more lucky diners since its recent facelift, 135-350.

● ◆◆ *Le Marcande*, 52, rue de Miromesnil, ☎ (1) 42.65.19.14, AE DC Visa ▥ ⟡ closed Sat and Sun, 1-26 Aug. The cuisine of this handsome restaurant is supervised by superchef Michel Lorain of Joigny's *Côte Saint-Jacques*, 180-320.

● ◆◆ *Les Thermes du Royal Monceau*, 39, av. Hoche, ☎ (1) 42.25.06.66, AE DC Visa ▥ ⟡ ♪ ▭ In the luxuriously sophisticated and over-equipped Roman baths, unlike any a real Roman might have seen, you can purchase a membership for a year or a day. The restaurant features pleasant, light fare by Thierry Couchot. Spec :

filet de turbot au sauternes et foie gras, éventail de magret de canard, soufflé léger au citron vert, 120-185.

● ◆◆ **Tong Yen**, 1 bis, rue Jean-Mermoz, ☎ (1) 42.25.04.23, AE DC Euro Visa, closed 1-25 Aug. A crowded Chinese spot, favoured by local celebrities whom Thérèse Luong greets warmly. Peking duck, 250.

● ◆◆ **Chez Vong**, 27, rue du Colisée, ☎ (1) 43.59.77.12, AE DC Visa Ⓟ ♪ closed Sun. A chic Chinese eatery with a Hollywood decor. Refined cuisine and the service can be very good indeed. Spec : Peking duck, Vietnamese dumplings *(banh cuon)*, sautéed crab Cantonese, 200.

● ◆◆ **Flora Danica**, 142, av. des Champs-Élysées, ☎ 43.59.20.41, AE DC Euro Visa ⚌ closed 24 Dec and 1 May. Danish salmon in all possible guises (smoked, marinated, grilled, etc), herring, 300.

● ◆◆ **Hédiard**, 21, pl. de la Madeleine, ☎ (1) 42.66.09.00, AE DC Euro Visa ♪ closed Sun. So you won't die of hunger or thirst. Take-out, gourmet shop, wines, 260.

● ◆◆ **L'Espace**, 1, av. Gabriel, ☎ (1) 42.66.11.70, AE DC Euro Visa, closed Sat noon. A high-class crush guaranteed daily, overseen by Jacques Collart : buffet, daily specials, pastries, inexpensive wines. Pierre Cardin lunches here on his home turf —how reassuring! Pianobar, 130-240.

● ◆◆ **La Ligne**, 30, rue Jean-Mermoz, ☎ (1) 42.25.52.65, DC Euro Visa ♪ closed Sat and Sun , Aug, 25-31 Dec. Cross the line *(la ligne)* to find excellent food by Jean Speyer, 185.

● ◆◆ **Le Drugstorien**, 1, av. Matignon, ☎ (1) 43.59.38.70, AE DC Visa The Publicis chain's very good restaurant : *foie gras frais maison, sole à la ciboulette*, 120-210.

◆◆ **Androuet**, 41, rue d'Amsterdam, ☎ (1) 48.74.26.90 A comeback for the restaurant of this shrine to French cheese. *Tourte au roquefort, croquettes Marie Harel* (she invented camembert), *raviolis de chèvre, fondues* (order in advance), 250-300.

◆◆ **Baumann-Marbeuf**, 15, rue Marbeuf, ☎ (1) 47.20.11.11, AE DC Euro Visa ♪ The place to come for good meat and *choucroute*, 170-200.

◆◆ **Copenhague**, 142, av. des Champs-Élysées, ☎ 43.59.20.41, AE DC Euro Visa ⅋ closed Sun and hols, 1 wk Jan, 2-30 Aug. Spec : salmon marinated with dill, reindeer steaks with blackberries in sweet-and-sour sauce, 340.

◆◆ **Le Vanillier**, 90, rue la Boétie, ☎ (1) 42.89.28.28, closed Sat and Sun. Excellent Malgasy cuisine, closer than Madagascar, 200.

● ◆ **Chez Tante Louise**, 41, rue Boissy-d'Anglas, ☎ (1) 42.65.06.85, AE DC Euro Visa, closed Sat and Sun, Aug. In this cosy setting, Bernard Lhiabastres serves enjoyable food that is bound to attract crowds to his handsome establishment. As always, pains are taken with the quality, choice and pricing of wines, 170-250.

● ◆ **Le Boeuf sur le Toit**, 34, rue du Colisée, ☎ (1) 43.59.83.80, AE DC Visa. If you don't mind waiting in line...oyster bar and irreproachably fresh seafood, 140-160.

● ◆ **Savy**, 23, rue Bayard, ☎ (1) 47.23.46.98, Visa, closed Sat and Sun, 1-30 Aug. Where radio personalities gather. It's good, simple and not too expensive. Cuisine of Auvergne : *choux aveyronnais, farçou, jambonneau aux lentilles*, 120-210.

◆ **Grand Pub Lady-Hamilton**, 82, av. Marceau, ☎ (1) 47.20.20.40, Visa ⟨ ♪ A fine English pub, known as the site of many a 'third half' for football players and fans, 70-110.

◆ **Le Bar des Théâtres**, 6, av. Montaigne, ☎ (1) 47.23.34.63, closed Aug. A hangout for television journalists. After-theatre suppers. More-than-decent *brasserie fare*, 150-200.

◆ **Le Bistrot de la Gare**, 73, av. des Champs-Élysées, ☎ (1) 43.59.67.83, Visa, 50-100.

◆ **Théâtre du Rond-Point**, av. F.-Roosevelt, ☎ (1) 42.56.22.01, Visa. Where the Renaud-Barrault theatre troupe meets after the show, 50-150.

PARIS IX

⊠ 75009

Hotels :

● ★★★★(L) *Scribe* (I.L.A., Sofitel), 1, rue Scribe, ☎ (1) 47.42.03.40, Tx 214653, AE DC Euro Visa, 217 rm 🏊 ᵴ 1490. Rest. ● ◆◆◆ *Les Muses* ♪ ᵴ closed Sat and Sun , aug and hols. A fresh, new decor and a young, new chef, Christian Massault, for this eminently agreeable hotel restaurant. Light, flavourful cuisine : *tagliatelle aux escargots et à la sauge, sole au vermouth, navarin de canette de Challans, délice de chocolat au coulis d'orange*, 160-220◆◆ *Le Jardin des Muses* ♪ ᵴ A coffee shop serving low-calorie specialties for the fitness-minded, 100.

★★★★(L) *Grand Hôtel*, 2, rue Scribe, ☎ (1) 42.68.12.13, 583 rm 12 apt ᵴ 1250. Rest. ◆◆◆ *Café de la Paix* A traditional spot for after the theatre or ballet, 250-330.

● ★★★ *Léman*, 20, rue de Trevise, ☎ (1) 42.46.50.66, Tx 281086, AE DC Euro Visa, 24 rm ♪ 🏊 An enchanting decor, peace and quiet, 650.

★★★ *Aston*, 12, cité Bergère, ☎ (1) 47.70.52.46, AE DC Euro Visa, 34 rm ⌕ ᵴ 450.

★★★ *Casino*, 41, rue de Clichy, ☎ (1) 48.74.74.99, AE Euro Visa, 40 rm, 225. Rest. ● ◆◆ ♪ closed Sat and Sun , hols. Chef J.-C. Jarrault presides in the kitchen, and is resposible for the delectable cuisine : *salade Christine, dos de sandre à la vapeur d'algues et aux queues de langoustines, tournedos 'Yella'*, 120-260.

★★★ *Franklin*, 19, rue Buffault, ☎ (1) 42.80.27.27, Tx 640988, AE DC Euro Visa, 64 rm ⌕ 🏊 490. Rest. ◆ ♪ closed Sat and Sun, 15 Jul-15 Aug, 150-200.

★★ *Résidence Sémard*, 15, rue Pierre-Semard, ☎ (1) 48.78.26.72, 41 rm ⌕ 210.

Moulin Rouge, 39, rue Fontaine, ☎ (1) 42.82.08.56, Tx 660055, AE DC Euro Visa, 50 rm ⌕ 🏊 480.

Restaurants :

● ◆◆◆◆ *Café de la Paix Opéra*, 3, pl. de l'Opéra, ☎ (1) 47.42.97.02, Tx 670738, AE DC Euro Visa ⚜ ᵴ closed Aug. Gil Jouanins' authentic "grande cuisine" is perfectly suited to Garnier's decor and frescoes : *petite nage froide de crustacés aux concombres et menthe poivrée, filet de canette poêlé aux petits légumes nouveaux, assiette aux trois cacaos*. Fine cellar, 350.

● ◆◆◆ *Charlot*, 12, place Clichy, ☎ 48.74.49.64 Seafood, shellfish, super-fresh fish in this, the jewel in the Blanc family's crown, superbly decorated by Pierre Pothier. Open until 2 am, 200.

● ◆◆ *La Table d'Anvers*, 2, pl. d'Anvers, ☎ (1) 48.78.35.21, Visa 🅿 Excellent quality here! They're young and talented, working in a modern decor, charging agreeably affordable prices. Who are they? Christian and Philippe Conticini. Father Roger oversees the dining room and the cellar (a little paradise for good bottles). *Salade tiède de moules, céleri et fenouil croquant au safran, rouget poêlé sur une fondue de pied de porc et céleri frais.* Dreamy desserts, original dishes, lots of spices, sweet-and-sour combinations, earthy fare..., 100-180.

● ◆◆ *Café de la Paix Relais Capucines*, 12, bd des Capucines, ☎ (1) 42.68.12.13, Tx 670738, AE DC Euro Visa ♪ ᵴ Classified frescoes by Charles Garnier adorn this pleasant winter garden. The traditional Burgundy cuisine overseen by Gil Jouanin is delicious. The terrace, the Foyer Bar Opéra open til 10pm, 150.

● ◆◆ *Cartouche-Edouard VII*, 18, rue Caumartin, ☎ (1) 47.42.08.82, AE Visa, closed Sun, 25 Jul-23 Aug. Hurray for the Southwest and its generous cuisine, served in this annex of the *Repaire de Cartouche. Confits, foie gras,* etc..., (served until 2am), 210.

● ◆◆ *Le Grand Café Capucines*, 4, bd des Capucines, ☎ (1) 47.42.75.77, AE DC Euro Visa 🅿 ⚜ ♪ ᵴ Open day and night, just like in the Belle Époque. Seafood and other delicious fare, 180.

◆◆ *Au Petit Riche*, 25, rue Le Peletier, ☎ (1) 47.70.68.68, AE Visa ♪ closed Sun, 1-27 Aug. This authentic turn-of-the-century bistro offers a wealth of good Loire Valley vintages, but the food needs some bucking up, 110-180.

♦♦ *Le Square*, 6, sq. de l'Opéra, ☎ (1) 47.42.78.50, AE Visa, closed Sat noon and Sun. An actors rendezvous. Lots of men - and a few pretty girls. Period woodwork and contemporary cuisine, 140-200.

♦♦ *Savoie-Bretagne*, 21, rue Saint-Lazare, ☎ (1) 48.78.91.94, Euro Visa, closed Sat and Sun , eves, 15-30 Aug. Spec : *cœur d'artichaut frais aux crevettes, filets de sole aux pâtes fraîches et au basilic, blanc de turbot au gratin*, 105-200.

♦♦ *Taverne Kronenbourg*, 24, bd des Italiens, ☎ (1) 47.70.16.64, Euro Visa Ⓟ ♪ ♿ An authentic Alsatian enclave on the busy Grands Boulevards. Spec : *haddock sur choucroute, pied de cochon grillé sauce béarnaise, brochette de lotte*. Music, 90-140.

● ♦ *Ty Coz*, 35, rue St-Georges, ☎ (1) 48.78.42.95, AE DC Visa, closed Mon and Sun. Sparkling seafood for genuine Breton cuisine, 220.

● ♦ *Bar Romain*, 6, rue Caumartin, ☎ (1) 47.42.98.04, AE DC Euro Visa ♪ ♿ closed Sun, 3-29 Aug. Where show-biz personalities gather to tuck into Paris's best steak tar-tare. Open until 2 am, 160.

♦ *Le Bœuf Bourguignon*, 21, rue de Douai, ☎ (1) 42.82.08.79 ♪ closed Sun, 3-17 Aug. Good, simple bistro featuring *bœuf bourguignon*. Ex-actors Nathalie Nattier and Robert Willar welcome you, 50-100.

♦ *Pagoda*, 50, rue de Provence, ☎ (1) 48.74.81.48, Visa, closed Sun in Aug. Spec : crab claws, sauteed shrimp, Peking duck, 55-150.

PARIS X

✉ 75010

Hotels :
★★★★ *Chamonix*, 8, rue d'Hauteville, ☎ (1) 47.70.19.49, Tx 641177, AE DC Euro Visa, 35 rm, 600.

★★★ *Gare du Nord*, 33, rue St-Quentin, ☎ (1) 48.78.02.92, AE Euro Visa, 49 rm ⌘ 370.

★★★ *National Hôtel*, 224, rue du Fbg-St-Denis, ☎ (1) 42.06.99.56, AE DC Euro Visa, 58 rm ♿ 340.

★★ *Baccarat*, 19, rue des Messageries, ☎ (1) 47.70.96.92, AE DC Euro Visa, 31 rm ⋙ 🏊 320.

★★ *Frantour-Château-Landon*, 3, rue de Château-Landon, ☎ (1) 42.41.44.88, AE DC Euro Visa, 161 rm ♿ 340.

Restaurants :
● ♦♦ *Au Chateaubriant*, 23, rue de Chabrol, ☎ (1) 48.24.58.94, AE Visa ℗ closed Mon and Sun , Aug, 1 wk in winter. For more than a decade, Guy Bürkli, that excellent chef, formerly with J. Forno, has been pre-paring pasta. Spec : *scampi fritti, paglia e fieno alla conta-dina, zabaglione al marsala*, Italian wines, 250.

● ♦♦ *Chez Michel*, 10, rue de Belzunce, ☎ (1) 48.78.44.14, AE DC Visa ℗ closed Fri and Sat , 15 days in Feb, 1-24 Aug. A master of classic cuisine, M. Tounissoux upholds the great traditions and prices... Spec : *salade de foie gras à l'effilochée d'endives, filet de bar sur fondue de tomates au basilic, fondant au choco-lat*, 300-400.

● ♦♦ *Le Louis XIV*, 8, bd St-Denis, ☎ (1) 42.08.56.56, AE DC Visa ℗ ♿ closed Mon and Tue, 31 May-1 Sep. A fine establishment serving cuisine in the grand tradition. The spit-roasted meats and charcoal grills are textbook examples of what such fare should be, 220-310.

● ♦♦ *Le New-Port*, 79, rue du Fbg-St-Denis, ☎ (1) 48.24.19.38, AE Visa ℗ 🏊 closed Mon and Sun, 2-24 Aug, 20 Dec-5 Jan. Fish and seafood get top billing : *charlotte de rougets, sole farcie à l'ail et tomate légère-ment anisée*, 200.

♦♦ *Brasserie Terminus-Nord*, 23, rue de Dunkerque, ☎ (1) 42.85.05.15, AE DC Visa. A Bucher *brasserie*, complete with turn-of-the-century decor : oysters all year round, *choucroute paysanne, gâteau glacé au caramel*, 100-140.

♦♦ *Casimir*, 6, rue de Belzunce, ☎ (1) 48.78.32.53, AE DC Euro Visa ℗ closed Sat noon and Sun. Classic dishes, as rich as the bill..., 140-240.

♦♦ *Julien*, 16, rue du Fbg-St-Denis, ☎ (1) 47.70.12.06, AE DC Visa. A long wait, but the welcome and service are quite capably handled. But careful! One meal brought us overcooked sole and mussels, nearly raw french fries. Keep an eye on things, Monsieur Bucher! Thank you, 105-140.

● ♦ *Brasserie Flo*, 7, cour des Petites-Ecuries, ☎ (1) 47.70.13.59, AE DC Visa, closed Aug. Chic, fashionable, up-to-the-minute and everyone waits in line. Uneven cuisine. Oyster and piano bars, 150-250.

● ♦ *La P'tite Tonkinoise*, 56, rue du Fbg-Poissonnière, ☎ (1) 42.46.85.98, Visa ♪ closed Mon and Sun, 1 Aug-15 Sep, 22 Dec-5 Jan. For the cognoscenti, one of the capital's best examples of Vietnamese cuisine, prepared by the Costa family : *nems*, stuffed crab, filet of goose or duck roasted with five flavours, 160.

♦ *Aux Deux Canards*, 8, rue du Faubourg-Poissonnière, ☎ 47.70.03.23 The first restaurant for non-smokers in Paris. More will surely follow. Classic cooking : Barbary ducks *à l'orange* or *au poivre vert*, 90-180.

PARIS XI

✉ 75011

Hotels :

★★★★ *Holiday Inn*, 10, pl. de la République, ☎ (1) 43.55.44.34, Tx 210651, AE DC Euro Visa, 333 rm Ⓟ ♪ 🏊 ⊗ 1280. Rest. ♦♦ *La Belle Epoque* ♪ ᾱ ⊗ 150-195 ; child : 45.

★★★ *Le Méridional*, 36, bd Richard-Lenoir, ☎ (1) 48.05.75.00, AE DC Euro Visa, 36 rm, 450.

★★ *Nord et de l'Est*, 49, rue de Malte, ☎ (1) 47.00.71.70, Visa, 44 rm ⊗ closed 25 Jul-1 Sep, 24 Dec-3 Jan, 210.

★★ *Royal Voltaire*, 53, rue Richard-Lenoir, ☎ (1) 43.79.75.67, AE DC Euro Visa, 55 rm, 230.

Restaurants :

● ♦♦ *A Sousceyrac*, 35, rue Faidherbe, ☎ (1) 43.71.65.30, AE Visa ⊗ closed Sat and Sun , Aug. Since 1923, good food has been a family affair with the Asfaux. It's delicious, not too expensive and generously served : *terrine de foie gras frais, ris de veau entier aux champignons*, cassoulet on Wed and Fri, 120-220.

● ♦♦ *Chez Philippe*, 106, rue de la Folie-Méricourt, ☎ (1) 43.57.33.78 Ⓟ closed Sat and Sun , Aug. Warm, friendly Philippe Serbource directs family members and charming colleagues. Rich, splendid Southwestern fare. The cellar is the boss's pride, 220.

● ♦♦ *Chez Fernand*, 17, rue de la Fontaine-au-Roi, ☎ (1) 43.57.46.25, closed Sat noon and Sun , Aug. Fernand is inspired by good things from Normandy : *raie au camembert, émincé de canard au cidre et pommes*, camemberts aged on the premises, *tarte aux pommes, crêpes*. The prices are modest, and the little fixed meal is nearly a giveaway, 85-150.

● ♦♦ *Le Péché Mignon*, 5, rue Guillaume-Bertrand, ☎ (1) 43.57.02.51, Visa ♪ ᾱ closed Mon and Sun , Aug, 1 wk at Easter. Cuisine in tune with the seasons and the tides : *mosaïque de trois poissons, panaché de poissons fins à la julienne de légumes, rouelles de ris de veau braisé*, 195.

● ♦♦ *Le Repaire de Cartouche*, 8, bd des Filles-du-Calvaire, ☎ (1) 47.00.25.86, AE Visa ᾱ closed Sun, 25 Jul-23 Aug. A fine place for Southwestern fare, 90-210.

● ♦ *Astier*, 44, rue J.-P.-Timbaud, ☎ (1) 43.57.16.35, Visa, closed Sat and Sun , Aug. Michel Picquart continues to watch over his kitchen and cellar, and to keep prices down, 95.

● ♦ *La Maison des Antilles (Restaumagre)*, pl. des Antilles, ☎ (1) 43.48.77.17, Tx 213810, AE DC 📺 ♪ ᾱ A market just like in the islands, an exotic *brasserie* dubbed *Les Quatre Vents*, and a restaurant, *Le Beauharnais*. Refresh your vacation memories, or just get to know Martinique, Guadeloupe, Guyana and the Réunion islands, 50-170.

♦ *Chez Paul*, 13, rue de Charonne, ☎ (1) 47.00.34.57, closed Sat and Sun , hols, Aug, 2 wks in Sep. M. and Mme Paul's generous cuisine, 70-120.

PARIS XII

⊠ 75012

Hotels :
★★★ *Azur*, 5, rue de Lyon, ☎ (1) 43.43.88.35, AE Visa, 62 rm, 360.
★★★ *Modern'Hôtel Lyon*, 3, rue Parrot, ☎ (1) 43.43.41.52, AE Visa, 53 rm ⅏ 385.
★★★ *Paris-Lyon Palace*, (Inter-Hôtel), 11, rue de Lyon, ☎ (1) 43.07.29.49, AE DC Euro Visa, 128 rm ⅃ 420.
★★★ *Terminus Lyon*, 19, bd Diderot, ☎ (1) 43.43.24.03,
★★ *Frantour-Gare de Lyon*, 2, Pl. Louis-Armand, ☎ (1) 43.44.84.84, Tx 217094, AE DC Euro Visa, 315 rm ⅃ 450.

Restaurants :
● ◆◆◆ *Au Pressoir*, 257, av. Daumesnil, ☎ (1) 43.44.38.21, Euro Visa Ⓟ closed Sat and Sun, Aug and Feb school hols. A brand-new decor, and delicious cuisine by Henri Seguin : *terrine de deux foies, bar en peau, ris de veau aux noix et au lard*, 280-300.
◆◆◆ *Le Train Bleu*, 20, bd Diderot, ☎ (1) 43.43.09.06, DC Euro Visa Ⓟ The landmark turn-of-the-century dining room is alone worth the trip ; the food is not, 195-230.
● ◆◆ *Trou Gascon*, 40, rue Taine, ☎ (1) 43.44.34.26, Visa Ⓟ ⅃ closed Sat and Sun, 15 Jul-15 Aug, 25 Dec-1 Jan. Now the annex of Alain Dutournier, installed rue Castiglione at the *Carré des Feuillants*, the *Trou Gascon* is in the capable hands of Mme Dutournier. Southwestern specialties : *raviolis de crabe au basilic, saumon rôti au chou tendre, cassoulet "Trou Gascon"*. Wonderful collection of Armagnacs, 250.

● ◆◆ *Epicure 108*, 22, rue Fourcroy, ☎ 47.63.34.00, Visa, closed Sat noon and Sun. Just 30 places here, their occupants carefully pampered by M. and Mme Pequignot : *spirale de poissons crus, lotte rôtie à la gentiane, rognonnade d'agneau, gâteau opéra chocolat à l'orange*. An elegant fixed-price offering available in the evening, 175.

● ◆◆ *La Gourmandise*, 271, av. Daumesnil, ☎ (1) 43.43.94.41, AE DC Visa Ⓟ ♪ ⅃ closed Sat noon and Sun, 12-19 Apr, 9-23 Aug. Alain Denoual is a worthy chef who deserves your encouragement : *salade d'épinards et de magret fumé, fricassée de langoustines en feuille de choux, agneau au miel*, 135-220.

◆◆ *La Tour d'Argent*, 6, pl. de la Bastille, ☎ (1) 43.49.90.32 The "other one". A pretty *brasserie* decorated by Slavik. Seafood, *choucroute*, moderate prices, 150.

PARIS XIII

⊠ 75013

Hotels :
★★ *Gobelins*, 57, bd St-Marcel, ☎ (1) 43.31.79.89, 45 rm, 280.
★★ *Résidence des Gobelins*, 9, rue des Gobelins, ☎ (1) 47.07.26.90, Tx 206566, AE DC Euro Visa, 32 rm ⌕ ♪ 280.
★★ *Véronèse*, 5, rue Véronèse, ☎ (1) 47.07.20.90, 66 rm ⅏ 170.

Restaurants :
● ◆◆◆ *Les Vieux Métiers de France*, 13, bd Auguste-Blanqui, ☎ (1) 45.88.90.03, AE DC Euro Visa ≪ ⌕ ♪ A talented and inventive chef, Michel Moisan. More than 1000 bottles in the cellar to go with his specialties : *cocotte d'oursins, turbotin belle Gabrielle, langoustines maraîchères*, 185-350.
● ◆◆ *Le Petit Marguery*, 9, bd de Port-Royal, ☎ (1) 43.31.58.59, AE DC Euro Visa, closed Mon and Sun, Aug, 24 Dec-2 Jan. The Cousin brothers shop, cook and run their restaurant with exemplary good humour : *wild mushrooms, game in season, coquilles Saint-Jacques*, 120-230.
● ◆◆ *Le Ti Koc*, 13, pl. de Vénitie, ☎ (1) 45.84.21.00, Visa. The Asian community's cabaret for the whole family. Music and singers, just like back home. Chinese food, *dim sum*, 200.

● ◆◆ *Les Algues*, 66, av. des Gobelins, ☎ (1) 43.31.58.22, AE Visa ℗ ⅙ closed Mon and Sun, 2-24 Aug, 20 Dec-5 Jan. Sparkling fresh fish : *nage de rougets, plie soufflée au crabe sauce basilic*, 90-200.
◆◆ *Chinatown Olympiades*, 44, av. d'Ivry, ☎ (1) 45.84.72.21, Euro Visa. Chic Chinese cooking at brasserie prices, 120-210.
◆◆ *Le Traiteur*, 28, rue de la Glacière, ☎ (1) 43.31.64.17, AE DC Euro Visa ℗ ⅗ ⅙ ✵ closed Sat and Sun, 1-20 May, 20 Dec-10 Jan. Classic cuisine with a terrace in fine weather, 90-175.
● ◆ *Hawaï*, 87, av. d'Ivry, ☎ (1) 45.86.91.90, Visa ♪ ✵ closed Thu. The Asiatic version of Lipp : a-see-and-be-seen brasserie. Spec : *soupe Tonkinoise*, beef *tau bay*, skewered shrimp, rice with spare ribs, 80.
◆ *Berges (Chez Jacky)*, 109, rue du Dessous-des-Berges, ☎ (1) 45.83.71.55 ⅗ ♪ closed Sat and Sun, 31 Jul-1 Sep. A friendly spot worth seeking out. The owner shops at the Rungis market, 250.

PARIS XIV

✉ 75014

Hotels :
★★★★(L) *Le Méridien Montparnasse*, 19, rue du Cdt-Mouchotte, ☎ (1) 43.20.15.51, Tx 200135, AE DC Euro Visa, 952 rm ℗ ⅗ ♪ ⅙ ♪ ⌁ ⌁ ♩ 1250. Rest. ● ⅗ *Le Montparnasse "25"* ♪ ✵ closed Sun, 3-31 Aug. Overseen by chef Raoul Gaïga, a real pro. In a 1920s setting, comfortable, contemporary food : *bourride à la provençale, dos de turbot rôti*, 195-400◆ *La Ruche* ⟨ ♪ ⅙ ✵ Open all day. Buffet until 10pm, 140-200 ; child : 70. ◆ *Le Park* ⟨ ♪ ⅙ (l.s.). In fine weather, dine in the pretty garden. Buffet, grills, barbecue. *Le Corail* - Piano-bar, 120-150.
★★★★(L) *Pullman Saint-Jacques* (ex P.L.M.), 17, bd St-Jacques, ☎ (1) 45.89.89.80, Tx 270740, AE DC Euro Visa, 797 rm ℗ ⅗ ♪ ⅗ 900. Rest. ◆ *Le Café Français* ♪ 160-215◆ *Le Patio* ♪ 100.
★★ *Le Châtillon*, 11, sq. de Châtillon, ☎ (1) 45.42.31.17, 31 rm ⅗ ⅙ closed Aug, 190.
★★ *Midi*, 4, av. René-Coty, ☎ (1) 43.27.23.25, 50 rm, 260.
★★ *Moulin Vert*, 74, rue du Moulin-Vert, ☎ (1) 45.43.65.38, Tx 260818, AE DC Euro Visa, 28 rm ⌂ ⅗ ♪ 290.

Restaurants :
● ◆◆◆ *Chez Albert*, 123, av. du Maine, ☎ 43.20.05.19, closed Fri eve and Sat. This is obviously a lucky restaurant (André Daguin, J.-P Vigato practiced here). Stéphane Pruvot knows his way around a kitchen, and his future looks bright. *Tête de veau ravigote, ris de veau poêlé*. Excellent meat, 250-300.
● ◆◆◆ *Le Duc*, 243, bd Raspail, ☎ (1) 43.22.59.59, Tx 204896, closed Mon, Sat, Sun. Depending on what's best and freshest at the Rungis market (the world's biggest port), Paul and Jean Minchelli serve a dazzling array of fresh fish and seafood. They 'invented' raw fish (sea bass, scallops, salmon) and lots of other good things : *rougets en vessie, sole au vinaigre, soupe tiède de langoustines*. Branches in Geneva and the Seychelles, 300-500.
● ◆◆◆ *Les Armes de Bretagne*, 108, av. du Maine, ☎ (1) 43.20.29.50, AE DC Euro Visa ℗ ⅗ ♪ ⅙ closed Mon and Sun eve ex hols, 4-31 Aug. Fine seafood in a Napoléon-III setting, 200-300.
● ◆◆ *Aux Iles Marquises*, 15, rue de la Gaîté, ☎ (1) 43.20.93.58, AE Visa ♪ ⅙ closed Sat noon and Sun. Mathias Thery, a Troisgros alumnus, presides in the kitchen. Hurry over to try his fish and seafood dishes before the neighbourhood is overrun (the *Bobino* just reopened!), 105-230.
● ◆◆ *Gérard et Nicole*, 6, av. Jean-Moulin, ☎ (1) 45.42.39.56, Visa ℗ closed Sat and Sun , wk of Aug 15. In a decor that they and their patrons admire, Gérard and Nicole are as friendly as ever, and their cooking just as delicious : *raviolis de langoustines, filets de rouget à l'huile d'olive*. Loire Valley wines, 250-280.
● ◆◆ *La Cagouille*, 10-12, place Brancusi, ☎ (1) 43.22.09.01, closed Mon and Sun, Jul. Everything

here is spanking new, including (especially) the luminously fresh fish purchased nightly at the Rungis wholesale food market. Owner Gérard Allemandou selects the engaging wines and prepares the simple, simply marvelous food. A Charentes native, he collects fine Cognacs - some date back to 1805! 250-300.

● ◆◆ *L'Assiette*, 181, rue du Château, ☎ (1) 43.22.64.86, AE DC Euro Visa, closed Mon and Tue. 'Lulu' has redecorated. Prices haven't risen in consequence, quality is high as ever, and portions of her excellent Béarnais cuisine are just as generous. Wear your *béret basque*, 180-230.

● ◆◆ *Lous Landès-Hervé Rumen*, 157, av. du Maine, ☎ (1) 45.43.08.04, Euro Visa ♪ ♿ closed Mon noon and Sun. Georgette has taken her well-deserved rest; now Hervé Rumen oversees the harmony of the kitchen and dining room. Hearty cuisine, 180-300.

● ◆◆ *La Chaumière des Gourmets*, 22, pl. Denfert-Rochereau, ☎ (1) 43.21.22.59, DC Euro Visa ℗ ⁓ 𝄢 closed Sat and Sun , 8-15 Mar, Aug. Freshened decor for Jean Becquet's delicious cuisine : *salade de ris de veau aux navets, marmite dieppoise*, game in season, 150-205.

● ◆◆ *Le Dôme*, 108, bd du Montparnasse, ☎ (1) 43.35.25.81, closed Mon. On the walls, 75 years' worth of photos record the history of this Montparnasse hot spot. Owner Claude Bras bought a nearby fish market to make sure his seafood is super-fresh. For a decade now, chef Paul Canal has cooked it expertly. Good wines, 200-300.

◆◆ *André Provost*, 1, rue de Coulmiers, ☎ (1) 45.39.86.99, AE Euro Visa ℗ closed Sat and Sun. Spec : *salade de pied de cochon, andouillette tirée à la ficelle, foie de veau au citron vert*, 260.

◆◆ *La Chaumière Paysanne*, 7, rue Léopold-Robert, ☎ (1) 43.20.76.55, AE DC Euro Visa ♿ ♪ ♿ closed Mon noon and Sun, 8-25 Aug. Didier Bondu's nicely executed cuisine changes often. Spec : *tartare de langouste, paupiette de lotte, pied de veau braisé au foie gras*, 150-220.

◆◆ *La Coupole*, 102, bd du Montparnasse, ☎ (1) 43.20.14.20, Euro Visa, closed Aug. A 1925 decor, picturesque patrons, and the food is quite good, 120-180.

◆◆ *La Guérite du Saint-Amour*, 209, bd Raspail, ☎ (1) 43.20.64.51 A *guérite* is a shelter, and this one is newly decorated. Fish is the specialty, and the Saint-Amour (a Beaujolais *cru*) flows, 120-230.

◆◆ *Le Moniage Guillaume*, 88, rue de la Tombe-Issoire, ☎ (1) 43.27.09.88, AE DC Euro Visa ℗ 𝄞 ♿ ♪ 5 rm, closed Sun. Spec : fish, seafood, shellfish (kept live in a tank), seafood *cassoulet*, 185-280.

◆◆ *Sarava*, 160, av. du Maine, ☎ (1) 43.22.23.64, AE DC Euro Visa ♪ closed Mon, 24 Dec-15 Jan. Brazilian atmosphere. Cuisine and service need improvement. 160-200.

● ◆ *Au Feu Follet*, 5, rue Raymond-Losserand, ☎ (1) 43.22.65.72 ♪ ♿ closed Sun and lunch, 18 Jul-18 Aug. A friendly little place where the hostess does the cooking. *Bœuf mode, brandade de morue* served until late at night, 140.

◆ *Le Bar à Huîtres*, 112, bd du Montparnasse, ☎ (1) 43.20.71.01, AE Visa ♪ Spec : seafood platter, *filet de turbot au caviar d'aubergines, choux à la crème chantilly*, 200.

◆ *Le Flamboyant*, 11, rue Boyer-Barret, ☎ (1) 45.41.00.22, closed Mon, Tue noon, Sun eve , Easter and Aug. The sun of the Antilles at your table, 150-250.

◆ *Léni Restaurant*, 7, rue Francis de Pressensé, ☎ (1) 45.41.06.17, closed Mon noon and Tue noon , Xmas school hols. Quite decent family-style food near a popular art film house, 110-130.

◆ *Les Petites Sorcières*, 12, rue Liancourt, ☎ (1) 43.21.95.68, Euro Visa, closed Mon, Sat noon, Sun , Aug, 1 wk at Xmas. Simple, pleasant cooking. Delightful reception. 70-150.

Be advised that hotels and restaurants in this Guide have perhaps changed addresses; prices indicated are also subject to modifications.

PARIS XV

⊠ 75015

Hotels :

★★★★(L) **Hilton International Paris**, 18, av. de Suffren, ☎ (1) 42.73.92.00, AE DC Euro Visa, 480 rm 29 apt P ⊱ ⚲ ⟨ ⚘ 1100. Rest. ◆◆◆ **Le Toit de Paris** ⊱ ⚘ closed Sun and at lunch, 27 Jul-28 Aug. A view of the Eiffel Tower comes free with the good cooking in this panoramic dining room, 235-325◆ **La Terrasse** Upgraded coffee-shop, 100-140◆ **Le Western** American meat cooked U.S.-style, 155-200.

★★★★(L) **Nikko**, 61, quai de Grenelle, ☎ (1) 45.75.62.62, 777 rm 9 apt P ⚲ ⚘ ⟥ 900. Rest. ● ◆◆◆ **Les Célébrités** ⚭ M. Poncet in the dining room and J. Sénéchal in the kitchen make an admirable team. The food is in the tradition of Joël Robuchon, who once headed up the kitchen here. Pastries by J.-P. Hévin, who took first prize in the French chocolate Olympics, 245-475◆◆ **Le Benkay** Traditional Japanese food and *teppenyaki* (food cooked on a hot steel burner), 120-210.

★★★★(L) **Sofitel Paris**, 8-12, rue Louis-Armand, ☎ (1) 45.54.95.00, Tx 200432, AE DC Euro Visa, 635 rm P ⚲ ♪ ⟥ A modern luxury hotel near the 'périphérique' highway, 850. Rest. ● ◆◆◆ **Le Relais de Sèvres** R. Durand is a modest but highly competent chef, as his cooking plainly shows. Spec : *saumon en carpaccio et petite friture d'encornets, saumon gratiné à la crème de noix, pruneaux glacés au mascara*, 240-350◆ **La Tonnelle** Simple, carefully cooked food, 110-250.

★★★ **Suffren La Tour**, 20, rue Jean-Rey, ☎ (1) 45.78.61.08, AE DC Euro Visa, 407 rm ⊱ ⚲ ⚭ 440. Rest. ◆◆ 150-210.

★★ **Lecourbe**, 28, rue Lecourbe, ☎ (1) 47.34.49.06, Tx 205440, AE DC Euro Visa, 47 rm ⚲ ♪ ⟁ 330.

★★ **Pacific Hôtel**, 11, rue Fondary, ☎ (1) 45.75.20.49, Euro, 66 rm, 240.

Restaurants :

● ◆◆◆◆ **La Maison Blanche**, 82, bd Lefèbvre, ☎ (1) 48.28.38.83, AE ♪ ⚭ closed Mon, Sat noon, Sun, 1-15 Sep. In a chic and sober off-white decor a bit larger than before, José Lampreia finally has room to move. Amid a riot of greenery and white blossoms he serves forth delicious specialties that delight his ever more numerous patrons. Surprisingly reasonable prices : *farcis d'oursin au pied de porc, tendron de veau aux épices, cabillaud au chou et lard, gâteau au chocolat*, 150-250.

● ◆◆◆◆ **Ravi**, 214, rue de la Croix-Nivert, ☎ (1) 45.31.58.09. The sumptuous, appetizing annex of Ravi Gupta. Just like the old days of the Raj. Spec : grills, 300.

● ◆◆◆ **Morot-Gaudry**, 6, rue de la Cavalerie, ☎ (1) 45.67.06.85, Visa ⊱ ⚲ closed Sat and Sun. With a picture-postcard view of the Eiffel Tower and the rooftops of Paris, Jean-Pierre Morot-Gaudry's is a captivating spot, where he will entice you with subtle cuisine and choice wines : over 600 different vintages, some available by the glass. *Mousseline d'huître au coulis de homard, crépinette de pieds aux pommes, roast* grouse (in season), 200-250.

● ◆◆◆ **Olympe**, 8, rue Nicolas-Charlet, ☎ (1) 47.34.86.08, AE DC Visa, closed Mon, Sat noon, Sun noon, 1-22 Aug, 22 Dec-4 Jan. Charming Dominique Nahmias now cooks lunches too. Evenings draw her fashionable fans who rave about creations like : *daurade aux artichauts et pommes de terre sautées à la sauge, terrine de pied de veau vinaigrette de poivrons tièdes*. Husband Albert oversees the list of pleasant little wines : white Burgundies, Côtes du Rhône, 180-420.

● ◆◆◆ **Pierre Vedel**, 19, rue Duranton, ☎ (1) 45.58.43.17 ⚘ closed Sat and Sun, 5 Jul-2 Aug, 24 Dec-3 Jan. In a bistro full of friends and acquaintances, chef Pierre Vedel (a weight-lifting buff) prepares fine classic dishes at moderate prices : *tête de veau, côte de bœuf aux champignons, blanquette d'huîtres de bouzigues* (in winter), *bourride*. Remarkable list of inexpensive wines, 180-250.

● ◆◆ **Aux Senteurs de Provence**, 295, rue Lecourbe, ☎ (1) 45.57.11.98, AE DC Euro Visa ⚭ closed Mon and

Sun. A new little spot for fresh fish, reasonably tariffed. Genuine *bouillabaisse, bourride, aïoli*, 135-210.
● ◆◆ *Aux Trois Horloges*, 73, rue Brancion, ☎ (1) 48.28.24.08, AE DC Euro Visa ♪ Genuine Franco-Algerian food just like his late mother used to make, prepared by Bernard Pons : *couscous, paëlla, méchoui, sepia, brochettes*. Home delivery, 150.
● ◆◆ *L'Aquitaine*, 54, rue de Dantzig, ☎ (1) 48.28.67.38, AE DC Euro Visa ♪ closed Mon and Sun. Seven young women, all capable cooks, serve forth fine Southwestern fare under the direction of Christiane Massia. *Petits gris d'Aquitaine, marmite du pêcheur aux fines herbes, faux-filet de Chalosse aux cèpes*. Regional wines, 300.
● ◆◆ *La Petite Bretonnière*, 2, rue de Cadix, ☎ (1) 48.28.34.39, AE Visa ♪ closed Sat noon and Sun, 3-24 Aug. Little by little, Alain Lamaison is building his nest, a very pretty one that sets off his cuisine to perfection, 230.
● ◆◆ *Restaurant du Marché*, 59, rue Dantzig, ☎ (1) 48.28.31.55, AE DC Euro Visa. The Massia family's first restaurant. Excellent, generous cuisine of the Landes region. Wines of Chalosse, Tursan, Madiran. Wine and food items to take out, 250.

● ◆◆ *Yvan Castex*, 15, rue Desnouettes, at the corner of 2, rue de Langeac, ☎ (1) 48.42.55.26, AE DC Euro Visa ♪ & closed Sun, 20-28 Feb, 10-31 Aug. Outstanding fare at utterly reasonable prices, 120-200.

● ◆◆ *Au Petit Mirabeau*, 3, rue de la Convention, ☎ (1) 45.77.95.79 ♪ closed Sat and Sun hols, 1 Jan, Aug, 25 Dec. Good, traditional fare by chef Bessière (*le Mouton Blanc*), 70-200.
● ◆◆ *La Gauloise*, 59, av. de la Motte-Picquet, ☎ (1) 47.34.11.64, AE DC Visa, closed Sat and Sun. Friendly spot, pleasant food, 250.
● ◆◆ *Le Clos de la Tour*, 22, rue Falguière, ☎ (1) 43.22.34.73, AE DC Euro Visa ♪ closed Sat noon and Sun, 3-26 Aug. A profusion of paintings and flowers, a short, well-designed menu, 240.

◆◆ *Bermuda Onion*, 16, rue Linois, ☎ (1) 45.75.11.11, AE DC Visa ♪ closed 1 May. P. Derderian's latest brainchild. American decor, with white sand on the terrace in summer. Beautiful girls, good food, 220.
◆◆ *Bistrot "121"*, 121, rue de la Convention, ☎ (1) 45.57.52.90, AE DC Euro Visa & closed Mon and Sun eve, 12 Jul-18 Aug, 20 Dec-1 Jan. A Parisian institution, in the Moussié family tradition, 190-350.
◆◆ *Chez Maître Albert*, 8-10, rue de l'Abbé-Groult, ☎ (1) 48.28.36.98, AE DC Euro Visa ♪ closed Mon. Pictures by Beaux-Arts students adorn the walls. Spec : *filets de sardines marinés au citron, bouillabaisse en filets*, 150-200.
◆◆ *Le Clos Morillons*, 50, rue des Morillons, ☎ (1) 48.28.04.37, Visa, closed Sat noon and Sun, 1-21 Jan. Pierre Vedel's old place is now home to a couple of worthy young restaurateurs : *terrine de lentilles vertes au foie gras, escalope de sandre*, 145-180.
◆◆ *L'Etape*, 89, rue de la Convention, ☎ (1) 45.54.73.49, Euro Visa ♪ closed Sat noon and Sun. Reasonably inexpensives, 110-220.
◆◆ *Marcel Prout*, 19, av. Félix-Faure, ☎ (1) 45.57.29.89, Visa, closed Sun. For lovers of Southwestern specialties, a restaurant with show-biz connections : *foie gras, salades au magret, confit*. Nicely chosen little Bordeaux wines, 120-150.
● ◆ *La Gitane*, 53 bis, av. de la Motte-Picquet, ☎ (1) 47.34.62.92, closed Sat and Sun. A real neighbourhood bistro, annex of *La Gauloise*. Patronized by journalists and politicians, 120-150.
● ◆ *Le Caroubier*, 8, av. du Maine, ☎ (1) 45.48.14.38, Visa, closed Mon and Sun, 15 Jul-2 Sep. All kinds of *couscous*. Good *merguez* sausages and *pastillas*, 120.
● ◆ *Le Volant*, 13, rue Béatrix-Dussane, ☎ (1) 45.75.27.67, Visa, closed Sat noon and Sun,

---

Be advised that hotels and restaurants in this Guide have perhaps changed addresses; prices indicated are also subject to modifications.

1-15 Aug. This friendly restaurant is the H.Q. of racing drivers. Warm, smiling young G. Houel dispenses tasty, robust cuisine : *foie de veau au vinaigre de xérès, pruneaux à l'orange*, 75-130.

● ◆ *Napoléon et Chaix*, 46, rue Balard, ☎ (1) 45.54.09.00, Visa ♦ ♪ 🕭 closed Sat noon and Sun , Aug. 'Dédé' Pousse takes time out between a film shoot and a cycling competition to help out his wife, Jocelyne, in their little restaurant. G. Magnan is in the kitchen : homemade pasta, catch of the day, 140-280.

◆ *L'Amanguier*, 51, rue du Théâtre, ☎ (1) 45.77.04.01, AE DC Visa ♪ closed 1 May. Quick service, tasty, inexpensive food. Other branches at Ternes, tel. 43.80.19.28 ; Neuilly, tel. 47.45.79.73 ; Richelieu, tel. 42.96.37.79, 130.

◆ *La Datcha Lydie*, 7, rue Dupleix, ☎ (1) 45.66.67.77, Visa ♦ ♪ 🕭 closed Wed, 15 Jul-31 Aug. A friendly Russian restaurant-cum-grocery : borscht, *chashlik*, smoked salmon, 90-150.

◆ *La Pastilla*, 7, rue d'Alençon, ☎ (1) 45.48.40.96 Moroccan specialties : excellent *couscous* and *pastilla*, 85-140.

◆ *Le Pacifico*, 50, bd du Montparnasse, ☎ (1) 45.48.63.87, closed Mon noon. Mexican food : *tacos, enchiladas, guacamole*, 80-120.

PARIS XVI

✉ 75016

Hotels :

★★★★(L) *Raphaël*, 17, av. Kléber, ☎ (1) 45.02.16.00, Tx 610356, AE DC Euro Visa, 87 rm ♦ ♪ 🐎 🕭 990. Rest. ◆◆ ♪ 🕭 180-250.

● ★★★★ (L) *St-James Club*, 5 pl. Chancelier-Adenauer, ☎ (1) 47.04.29.29, Tx 643850, AE DC Euro Visa, 38 rm Ⓟ ♦ ꣑ How times change ! Admission requirements to the St-James Club also Henceforth they are open with rooms and suites discreetly decorated by Renée Putman who has greated one of the Capital's loveliest residences. Billiards, sauna, gym, 2 000. Rest. ● ◆◆◆◆ Quality cuisine restricted to hotel guests and club members, 220-400.

★★★★ *Alexander*, 102, av. Victor-Hugo, ☎ (1) 45.53.64.65, Tx 610373, 62 rm ꣑ ⟋ 710.

★★★★ *Baltimore*, 88 bis, av. Kléber, ☎ (1) 45.53.83.33, Tx 611591, AE DC Euro Visa, 119 rm, 1080. Rest. ● ◆◆◆ *L'Estournel*, closed Sat and Sun , Aug. For your pleasure, a disciple of J. Robuchon is at work in the kitchen : *raviolis de crabe à l'orange, Saint-Pierre en habit vert au velouté de pistaches*, 185-350.

★★★★ *Résidence du Bois* (R.C.), 16, rue Chalgrin, ☎ (1) 45.00.50.59, 19 rm ꣑ ♦ 1000.

★★★ *la Muette*, 32, rue de Boulainvilliers, ☎ (1) 45.25.13.08, AE DC Euro Visa, 13 rm ꣑ ♦ ♪ 380.

★★ *Villa d'Auteuil*, 28, rue Poussin, ☎ (1) 42.88.30.37, 17 rm, 195.

Restaurants :

● ◆◆◆◆ *Faugeron*, 52, rue de Longchamp, ☎ (1) 47.04.24.53, closed Sat and Sun , Aug, 24 Dec-2 Jan. Three cheers! And our sincere congratulations. For the second consecutive time, a French sommelier is named 'world champion' : J.-C. Jambon. For more than a decade, he has capably administered *Faugeron's* exceptional cellar, where affordable bottles are also to be found. Guests are welcomed by the charming Gerlinde, and chef Henri Faugeron combines flavours and scents in an ideal symphony of which the Corrèze region provides the earthy notes. What a team! *Œufs coque à la purée de truffes, cervelas de ris de veau, filet de bœuf fumé à la vinaigrette de champignons, sablés à l'anis et aux framboises*. Business lunches, 350-400.

● ◆◆◆◆ *Jamin*, 32, rue de Longchamp, ☎ (1) 47.27.12.27, AE DC Visa ♪ closed Sat and Sun, Jul. What else can we say about gifted Joël Robuchon, the vice-president of our chefs'panel, about his capable and charming wife Janine, his peerless young brigade, the dining-room staff directed by J.-J. Kement, a tight team if ever there was one. We can only urge you to reserve (far in advance), and rejoice at the treat in store : *gelée de caviar à la crème de chou-fleur, galette de truffes aux oignons et lard fumé, agneau pastoral aux herbes en salade.* Great wines of course, but you'll find inexpensive bottles too, 420.

● ◆◆◆◆ *Jean-Claude Ferrero*, 38, rue Vital, ☎ (1) 45.04.42.42, AE DC Visa ⬜ ⬭ ⬯ closed Sat and Sun, 15 Aug-8 Sep, 24 Dec-5 Jan. It's like a breath of the country in Paris : a cosy little town house entirely redone by J.-C. Ferrero who, when he's not supervising the remaining workmen, performs his instinctive culinary magic in the kitchen. A knowledgeable mycologist, Ferrero serves a staggering array of truffles and mushrooms all year round. Andrée extends a smiling welcome. Garden dining room, private rooms, 350-400.

● ◆◆◆◆ *La Grande Cascade*, Bois de Boulogne, ☎ (1) 45.27.33.51, AE DC Visa ⬜ ⬭ ⬯ closed eves (15 Oct-15 Apr), 20 Dec-20 Jan. Napoléon III has abandoned his hunting lodge, but André Menut and his brigade have attracted a very posh crowd of clients to fill the gap. Jean Sabine presides over the kitchen. Splendid cellar and lovely terrace for summer days, 195-400.

● ◆◆◆◆ *Le Pré Catelan*, rte de Suresnes, Bois de Boulogne, ☎ (1) 45.24.55.58, DC Euro Visa Ⓟ ⬜ ⬭ ⬯ closed Mon and Sun eve, 5 Feb-3 Mar. A tireless globetrotter, Gaston Lenôtre's thoughts are never far from his cherished Pré Catelan, capably managed by his wife, Colette. When the sun shines, it's paradise, 480-500.

● ◆◆◆◆ *Le Vivarois*, 192, av. Victor-Hugo, ☎ (1) 45.04.04.31, AE DC Visa Ⓟ ⬭ ⬜ ⬯ closed Sat and Sun , Aug. Attention, please! We are here in a shrine to gustatory pleasures. A high priest of seasonal cooking, Claude Peyrot firmly believes in buying fresh foodstuffs at the Rungis market, as his appetizing menu attests : *coquilles Saint-Jacques saisonnières en crème de Noilly, poissons au gré de la marée, queue de bœuf au vin rouge.* Luscious pastries, and a wealth of wines, 255-450.

● ◆◆◆ *Le Petit Bedon*, 38, rue Pergolèse, ☎ (1) 45.00.23.66, Visa ♪ closed Sat and Sun , Aug. His many satisfied customers have not swelled Christian Ignace's head. He remains a capable, modest chef, who avoids fads and trends. Be sure to reserve a table : *tourteau frais tante Louise, pigeon au vinaigre de miel, filet de sole au coulis de moules et morilles,* 300.

● ◆◆◆ *Le Toit de Passy*, 94, av. Paul-Doumer, ☎ (1) 45.25.91.21, Visa Ⓟ ⬭ ♪ ⬯ closed Sat noon and Sun, 20 Dec-13 Jan. A superb restaurant in the sky, with a lovely outdoor terrace that affords an unbeatable view of the Eiffel Tower. The site inspires chef Yann Jacquot who is very nearly one of the city's best chefs : *soupe d'huîtres au jus de truffes et à l'aneth, langoustines rôties au beurre d'agrume, pigeonneau en croûte de sel.* Exceptional cellar, cigars, 170-300.

● ◆◆◆ *Michel Pasquet*, 59, rue La Fontaine, ☎ (1) 42.88.50.01, AE DC Euro Visa ⬭ ♪ ⬯ closed Sat noon and Sun, 14 Jul-15 Aug. Still the same excellent cuisine and service by members of the family. The elegant new decor is a plus, 160-300.

● ◆◆◆ *Patrick Lenôtre*, 28, rue Duret, ☎ (1) 45.00.17.67, Euro Visa ⬯ closed Sat and Sun, 15 Jul-5 Aug. At last he has his own restaurant, carrying on his family's tradition, 400-450.

● ◆◆◆ *Paul Chêne*, 123, rue Lauriston, ☎ (1) 47.27.63.17, AE DC Visa Ⓟ closed Sat and Sun, 30 Jul-2 Sep. This restaurant is as solid as an oak, and its wonderful cuisine never goes out of style. In fact, it appears to be coming back into fashion. What a treat to sit down in this pleasant room to a generously served meal. *Maquereaux frais au muscadet, terrine, rognon de veau aux trois moutardes, beignets de pomme, gelée de groseilles.* Appealing wines, 300-350.

● ◆◆◆ *Prunier-Traktir*, 16, av. Victor-Hugo, ☎ (1) 45.00.89.12, AE DC Euro Visa, closed Mon and Tue. Fresh fish served in the 1925 decor, at the bar or to take out. Quality and tradition, 220-360.

● ◆◆◆ *Ramponneau*, 21, av. Marceau, ☎ (1) 47.20.85.40, AE DC Euro Visa ⬭ closed Aug. Stylish and solid. *Terrine, œuf cocotte, côte de bœuf, gigot, charlotte au chocolat.* Fine wines, 350.

● ◆◆◆ *Shogun*, the *Nomadic*, port Debilly,

☎ (1) 47.20.05.04, AE DC Euro Visa ♪ ♿ ♒ Europe's biggest Japanese restaurant floats aboard the *Nomadic*. At night, an unforgettable view of the illuminated Eiffel Tower. A guaranteed change of pace : *sashimi, sushi, tempura, teppanyaki, saké* and kimonos. Prices according to the value of the yen, 130-550.

♦♦♦ *Ile de Kashmir*, quai Debilly, accross from 32, av. de New-York, ☎ (1) 47.23.50.97, AE DC Euro Visa Ⓟ ♪ ♒ Two floating restaurants : *Le Lotus and Le Jardin de Shalimar*. Arabian nights setting, Kashmiri cuisine, 125-230.

♦♦♦ *Le Chandelier*, 4, rue Paul-Valéry, ☎ (1) 47.04.55.22, AE DC Visa ♨ ♪ closed Fri and Sat noon , Sat eve Apr-Sep. Luxurious kosher restaurant in an 18thC town house, supervised by the Paris Beth-Din. Light dishes, 230-350.

● ♦♦ *Le Conti*, 72, rue Lauriston, ☎ (1) 47.27.74.67, AE Visa, closed Sat and Sun. Michel Ranvier, a Troisgros alumnus, fixes fabulous pasta, 250.

● ♦♦ *Le Mouton Blanc*, 40, rue d'Auteuil, ☎ (1) 42.88.02.21, Euro Visa ♪ ♿ closed 20 Jul-20 Aug. A literary shrine, formerly frequented by Molière and Boileau, where chef Bessières serves a food-lover's feast of quality fare at low prices : *panaché de saucisson, salade de moules, rognons d'agneau*. Fixed-price starter and main course option, 110-170.

● ♦♦ *Le Relais d'Auteuil*, 31, bd Murat, ☎ (1) 46.51.09.54, AE DC Euro Visa ♪ ♿ closed Sat noon and Sun. Patrick Pignol serves light, youthful, inspired cuisine. Sampling menu, fine wines, 150-250.

● ♦♦ *Pantagruel*, 11, rue de la Tour, ☎ 45.20.09.31, closed Sun. A new home for Christiane and Freddy Israel. Classic, copious dishes : *escargots en cassolette, foie de canard chaud aux myrtilles, turbot au Bouey*, game in season, 250-300.

● ♦♦ *Sous l'Olivier*, 15, rue Goethe, ☎ (1) 47.20.84.81, Visa ♬ ♨ closed Sat and Sun , hols. The young chef's efforts make this an agreeable place to pause for a meal : *émincé de paleron braisé à la roquette, rable de lapereau au gratin de champignons*, 130-220.

● ♦♦ *Chalet des Iles*, Lac Inférieur, Bois de Boulogne, ☎ (1) 45.88.04.69, DC Visa Ⓟ ♬ ♿ closed 30 Nov-1 Mar. For canoe buffs ; a real change of scene deep in the Bois de Boulogne. Very pleasant, 130-200.

● ♦ *Aux Trois Obus*, 120, rue Michel-Ange, ☎ (1) 46.51.22.58, Visa A friendly neighbourhood *brasserie* where sports fans gather. Wines chosen by the owner, oyster bar in winter, 150-250.

● ♦ *Brasserie le Stella*, 133, av. Victor-Hugo, ☎ (1) 47.27.60.54, closed 1 wk in Feb and Aug. Chic *brasserie* for power brokers, likable yet furiously fashionable. The owner buys his wines direct from the growers, 160-210.

PARIS XVII

✉ 75017

Hotels :
★★★★(L) *Concorde La Fayette*, 3, pl. du Gal-Koenig, ☎ (1) 47.58.12.84, Tx 650892, AE DC Euro Visa, 1000 rm Ⓟ ♪ ♪ 1200. Rest. ♦♦♦ *L'Etoile d'Or* ♪ ♿ Spec : *tartare de poissons fins au caviar*, 210-320. ♦♦ *L'Arc-en-Ciel* In fine weather, the terrace *le Barbecue*, 150-200.
★★★★(L) *Méridien Paris*, 81, bd Gouvion-St-Cyr, ☎ (1) 47.58.12.30, AE DC Euro Visa, 1027 rm 16 apt Ⓟ Chef Brazier can be proud of his team, 1000. Rest. ● ♦♦♦ *Le Clos Longchamp*, closed Sat and Sun. Featuring J.-M. Huard's light specialties : *filet de lotte et son foie avec algues et pistou, mignon de veau glacé "Orloff"*, 180-360. ● ♦♦ *Le Yamato* For regulars and numerous Japanese tourists, 100-160. ♦ *La Maison Beaujolaise* Wash down hearty *charcuterie* with cool Beaujolais, 140-220. ♦ *Le Café Arlequin* An excellent *brasserie*, 100-160. ♦ *Salle Lionel Hampton* ♪ The loss of our friend, the late, lamented Moustache is irreplaceable, but the good jazz keeps rolling along, just as he would

have wanted. Every Sun from noon to 3 pm, 'Jazz sur Brunch', big band and an abundant buffet, 230 ; child : 115.

★★★★ **Splendid Etoile**, 1, av. Carnot, ☎ (1) 47.66.41.41, Tx 280773, 57 rm ℗ ⌕ ⌕ ⌕ ✈ 690. Rest. ♦♦ ⌕ ⌕ closed Sat and Sun , Aug, 250.

● ★★★ **Regent's Garden**, (Mapotel), 6, rue Pierre-Demours, ☎ (1) 45.74.07.30, Tx 640127, AE DC Euro Visa, 40 rm ℗ ⌕ ⌕ ⌕ Pleasure of a blooming garden in a Napoléon-III residence, 600.

★★★ **Belfast**, 10, av. Carnot, ☎ (1) 43.80.12.10, AE DC Euro Visa, 54 rm ℗ ⌕ ⌕ At the foot of the Arch of Triumph, 450.

★★★ **Etoile Pereire** (R.S.), 146, bd Pereire, ☎ (1) 42.67.60.00, Tx 305551, AE DC Euro Visa, 26 rm ℗ ⌕ ✈ 520.

★★ **Prima Hôtel**, 167, rue de Rome, ☎ (1) 46.22.21.09, AE Visa, 30 rm, 240. Rest. ♦ 80-100.

★★ **Résidence Villiers**, 68, av. de Villiers, ☎ (1) 42.27.18.77, Tx 642613, 28 rm, 255.

Restaurants :

● ♦♦♦♦ **Michel Rostang**, 20, rue Rennequin, ☎ (1) 47.63.40.77, Tx 649629, Visa ℗ closed Sat and Sun, 1-18 Aug. Michel Rostang thrives in Paris, as does his pretty wife. Their new decor is a most attractive setting for his perfectly executed, inventive cuisine : canette de Bresse au sang, œufs de caille en coque d'oursin (Oct-Mar), filet de sole vapeur au persil, 200-550. ● ♦♦ **Bistrot d'à Côté**, 10, rue Gustave-Flaubert, ☎ 42.67.05.81. In a turn-of-the-century grocery store, Michel and Marie-Claude Rostang have opened a bistro featuring Lyonnais specialties, 180.

● ♦♦♦ **Alain Morel**, 143, av. de Wagram, ☎ (1) 42.27.61.50, closed Sat noon and Sun. A calm, sober setting in a prestigious neighbourhood worthy of chef Morel's talent. In fine weather, enjoy his light, inspired cuisine on the magnificent terrace. Salade de pommes de terre au foie gras, pudding à la moelle, côte de boeuf, millefeuille. Appealing wines, 250-400.

● ♦♦♦ **Apicius**, 122, av. de Villiers, ☎ (1) 43.80.19.66, AE Visa ℗ closed Sat and Sun, 30 Jul-30 Aug. The new darling of Parisian gourmets, J.-P. Vigato is without doubt a chef on the rise. We welcome him to our chefs'panel. Lucky man : he has a lovely wife and a very pretty restaurant. Fish and abats are the house specialties, Tête de veau remoulade, pied de porc rôti aux cèpes. Interesting wines, 250-300.

● ♦♦♦ **Guy Savoy**, 18, rue Troyon, ☎ (1) 43.80.40.61, Euro Visa, closed Sat and Sun, 15-31 Jul. In the former Bernardin restaurant Guy Savoy (C.S. H.C.F.) continues to offer his excellent cuisine in a new decor. M. Savoy proposes some excellent choices : poêlée de moules aux champignons du moment, pommes de terre et lotte rôties à l'échalotte confite, 400-450.

● ♦♦♦ **La Barrière de Clichy**, 1, rue de Paris, ☎ (1) 47.37.05.18, DC Euro Visa, closed Sat noon and Sun, 7-21 Aug. Gifted chef Yves Le Gallès is on his own now, in a fresh, bright decor : émincé de champignons aux choux, ris de veau aux escargots, 250-350.

● ♦♦♦ **Le Manoir de Paris**, 6, rue Pierre-Demours, ☎ (1) 45.72.25.25, AE DC Euro Visa ℗ ⌕ closed Sat and Sun, 6 Jul-3 Mar. The new decor signed Pierre Pothier is a much-needed improvement. Francis Vandenhende and his wife, Denise Fabre, now own a fresh, inviting restaurant, a perfect setting for Philippe Groult's fine cooking : rissoles de lotte aux épices, soupe de homard aux herbes fraîches, pied de porc rieuse à la sauvage. Appealing wines. Coming soon : a Niçois eatery on the upper floor, 250-300.

● ♦♦♦ **Ma Cuisine**, 18, rue Bayen, ☎ (1) 45.72.02.19, AE Euro Visa ℗ ⌕ ♪ closed Sat noon and Sun. René Sourdeix succeeds Alain Donnard, 205-300.

● ♦♦♦ **Paul et France**, 27, av. Niel, ☎ (1) 47.63.04.24, AE DC Visa, closed Sat and Sun, 14 Jul-15 Aug. Honorary Chef to the Paris soccer team, jovial Georges Romano accompanies the players to all official 'away' matches. A former footballer himself, Romano knows all about competition. He is a fierce defender of fine cuisine, and we are

happy to welcome him as a new member of our chefs'
panel. Light, spontaneous creations in tune with the seasons : *raviolis de tourteaux, filet de Saint-Pierre aux
coques, pigeon de ferme rôti*. Good wines and Armagnacs. A true southerner, the chef always has a good
story to tell, 300.

● ◆◆◆ *Sormani*, 4, rue du Gal-Lanrezac,
☎ (1) 43.80.13.91, Visa, closed Sat and Sun, 18-25 Apr,
2-22 Aug, 23 Dec-4 Jan. In a setting of blue velvet, under
the watchful eyes of a plaster Caesar, Pascal Fayet prepares first-rate Italian cuisine, including a gourmet array
of pasta : *raviolis, lasagne, spaghettis...* and of course
carpaccio, jambon, rouget, served with a carefully chosen
list of Italian wines, 300.

● ◆◆ *Auberge de Recoules*, 150, bd Pereire,
☎ (1) 43.80.63.22, AE DC Euro Visa ♿ closed Sat and
Sun , Aug. When you go in, you see it's really a bistro
chic. Simple but high-quality cuisine prepared by Bernard
Maire : seafood, remarkable *foie gras*, delicious *andouillette* and very good meats at affordable prices. To satisfy
his patrons, owner Pierre Le Hors plans to redeco-
rate, 200-250.

● ◆◆ *Chez la Mère Michel*, 5, rue Rennequin,
☎ (1) 47.63.59.80, Visa, closed Sat and Sun , Aug. The
true believer's temple of *beurre blanc*, whipped up by M.
Gaillard in his genuine little bistro, 240.

● ◆◆ *Chez Laudrin*, 154, bd Pereire, ☎ (1) 43.80.87.40,
AE Euro Visa, closed Sat and Sun. Jacques Billaud, aided
and abetted in his new decor by young Jean Jouhanneau
serves hearty fare along with tasty wines and Champagne
- you are billed only for what you drink : fish, kidneys, tripe,
rabbit, 250-300.

● ◆◆ *La Braisière*, 54, rue Cardinet, ☎ (1) 47.63.40.37,
Visa, closed Sat and Sun , Aug. Very nice food by talented
B. Vaxelaire : *farci de barbue au crabe, délice à la rhu-
barbe*, 175-230.

● ◆◆ *La Côte de Bœuf*, 4, rue Saussier-Leroy,
☎ (1) 42.27.73.50, AE DC Visa, closed Sat and Sun,
2 Aug-1 Sep. Beef of course, but try the daily specials too,
or the seasonal game and the *confits*, all beautifully prepared by S. Delmond, 150.

● ◆◆ *Lajarrige*, 16, av. de Villiers, ☎ (1) 47.63.25.61 ♪
closed Sat noon and Sun, 4 Aug-1 Sep. J.-C. Lajarrige
welcomes you into his 17thC decor like the musketeer he
is. Southwestern specialties executed by E. Marrottaf, a
disciple of André Daguin : *magret de mulard, brandade de
morue, grand cassoulet Lajarrige*, 115-185.

● ◆◆ *La Petite Auberge*, 38, rue Laugier,
☎ (1) 47.63.85.51, DC Euro Visa Ⓟ closed Mon and Sun,
3 Aug-1 Sep. No words can suffice to describe Léo Har-
bonnier's delightful cooking. Go see for yourself. Fabulous *millefeuille*, 180-250.

● ◆◆ *La Toque*, 16, rue de Tocqueville,
☎ (1) 42.27.97.75, Visa ♪ closed Sat and Sun,
10 Jul-10 Aug, 23 Dec-5 Jan. Young, talented Jacky Jou-
bert keeps a lid on the prices here. Spec : *escalope de
saumon poêlée, cuisse et râble de lapereau au chou*, 170.

● ◆◆ *Le Gouberville*, 1, pl. Charles-Fillion,
☎ (1) 46.27.33.27, Visa ⊰ ♧ ♪ closed Mon and Sun,
1-18 Aug. Discreet, provincial charm in the capital. A
church, a square and a terrace surrounded by summer
greenery. In the pretty dining room, a homey air prevails.
Foie gras frais maison, marmite dieppoise, 90-200.

● ◆◆ *Le Petit Colombier*, 42, rue des Acacias,
☎ (1) 43.80.28.54, Visa Ⓟ closed Sat and Sun noon,
1-17 Aug. A businessman as well as a chef (he heads up
the restaurateurs' union), Bernard Fournier practices his
craft with brio in a rustic, family-style inn where he keeps
a close eye on everything, especially the generous leg
of lamb carved tableside, calf's liver, honestly priced,
180-250.

● ◆◆ *Le Relais d'Anjou*, 15, rue de l'Arc-de-Triomphe,
☎ (1) 43.80.43.82, DC Visa ♧ ♪ closed Sat noon and Sun,
20 Jun-17 Jul. Outstanding example of Anjou's regional
cuisine. The owner, a real perfectionist, makes his own
rillettes. Wonderful wines, 200.

● ◆◆ *Le Santenay*, 75, av. Niel, ☎ (1) 42.27.88.44, AE
DC Euro Visa ⊰ ♧ ♪ closed Mon and Sun eve, 1-20 Aug.

In a pleasant Napoléon-III decor, Francis Vallot serves traditional cooking; his wife provides smiles and lovely bouquets. Spec : *brochet maraîchère*, great red Bordeaux and Burgundies, 250.

● ♦♦ *Michel Comby*, 116, bd Péreire, ☎ (1) 43.80.88.68, AE DC Visa P & closed Sat and Sun (open Sat eve Jun-Oct), 23 Feb-16 Mar, 20 Jul-2 Aug. Candlelight and flowers for Michel Comby, happy to be in his own place at last, after years of service at *Lucas Carton*. Here, he expresses his talent freely, to loud applause : *feuilleté de grenouilles au confit de poireaux, cassolette d'escargots chablisienne, rognons de veau*, 135-300.

● ♦♦ *Andrée Baumann*, 64, av. des Ternes, ☎ (1) 45.74.16.66, AE DC Euro Visa ♪ & Delicious *choucroute* in myriad guises : Alsatian, fish, Oriental, with boiled beef, etc...Oyster bar in winter, 100-200.

● ♦♦ *Chez Georges*, 273, bd Pereire, ☎ (1) 45.74.31.00, Visa, closed Aug. Georges Mazarguil maintains his tradition of excellent daily specials; meats carved at your table : *gigot rôti aux flageolets, petit salé aux choux*, 160-220.

● ♦♦ *Chez Guyvonne*, 14, rue de Thann, ☎ (1) 42.27.25.43, Visa ♪ closed Sat and Sun, 10 Jul-3 Aug, 24 Dec-5 Jan. In a peaceful spot near the parc Monceau, refined cuisine. Spec : *émincé de rognons de veau au vin de cornas*, 240.

● ♦♦ *Épicure 108*, 22 rue Foureroy, ☎ (1) 47.63.34.00, Visa closed Sat. noon and Sun. Just 30 places here, their occupants carefully pampered by M. and Mme Pequignot. *Spirale de poissons crus, lotte rôtie à la gentiane, rognonnade d'agneau, gâteau opéra, chocolat à l'orange*. An elegant fixed-price offering avalaible in the evening, 250.

● ♦♦ *La Coquille*, 6, rue du Débarcadère, ☎ (1) 45.72.10.73, AE Visa, closed Mon and Sun , 1 Jan, Aug, Xmas. C. Lansecker continues in the fine tradition of Paul Blache. Fresh shellfish in season, 300.

● ♦♦ *La Soupière*, 154, av. de Wagram, ☎ (1) 42.27.00.73, AE Euro Visa, closed Sat and Sun, 7-23 Aug. Outstanding soups by C. Thuillart, 130-180.

● ♦♦ *Michel Clave*, 10, rue Villebois-Mareuil, ☎ (1) 45.73.29.30 After the *Crillon*, the *Bristol* and the *Café de la Paix*, experienced chef Michel Clave has settled down here to serve you delightful dishes like *crêpes d'oeufs brouillés, blanquette de turbot, glace au chocolat amer*, 250.

● ♦♦ *Pétrus*, 12, pl. du Mal-Juin, ☎ (1) 43.80.15.95, AE DC Euro Visa P closed Mon and Sun , Aug. Oyster bar, excellent fish prepared by G. Dugast. *Navarin de homard, petite marmite du pêcheur à la nage*. Impressive cellar supervised by Jean Frambourt, president of the Sommeliers de France, 300.

● ♦ *Le Beudant*, 97, rue des Dames, ☎ (1) 43.87.11.20, AE DC Visa P ♪ closed Sat noon and Sun. Tiny, but the regionally inspired cuisine is tasty and well prepared : *foie gras frais maison*, fish, 200-280.

● ♦ *Pommeraie Jouffroy*, 36, rue Jouffroy, ☎ (1) 42.27.39.41, AE DC Visa P ♪ closed Sun , Aug. Norman cuisine in all its glory : cider, Calvados, *gratin de pomme*, 120-220.

♦ *Dessirier*, 9, pl. du Mal-Juin, ☎ (1) 43.80.50.72, DC Euro Visa P Superb oyster bar all year round, fish prepared the old-fashioned way, 250-350.

♦ *L'Amanguier*, 43, av. des Ternes, ☎ (1) 43.80.19.28, AE DC Visa ♪ closed 1 May, 130.

PARIS XVIII

✉ 75018

Hotels :

● ★★★★ *Terrass* (Mapotel), 12, rue Joseph-de-Maistre, ☎ (1) 46.06.72.85, Tx 280830, AE DC Euro Visa, 108 rm ⦗ 🛴 620. Rest. ♦♦ *La Guerlande* ♪ & At the foot of Montmartre, reliable cooking, 180. ♦ *L'Albaron* Fast service until 1am, 75-130.

★★★ *Résidence Montmartre*, 10, rue Burcq, ☎ (1) 46.06.45.28, Visa, 46 rm In a typical street of Old Montmartre, 240.

● ★★ *Tim Hôtel Montmartre*, 11, pl. Émile-Goudeau,

☎ (1) 42.55.74.79, Tx 650508, AE DC Euro Visa, 63 rm
⚘ ♪ 🐎 On a charming tree-shaded square, 295.
★★ *Capucines Montmartre*, 5, rue Aristide-Bruant,
☎ (1) 42.52.89.80, Tx 205139, AE DC, 30 rm ⚘ ♪ 250.
★★ *Prima-Lepic*, 29, rue Lepic, ☎ (1) 46.06.44.64,
Tx 281162, Visa, 38 rm ♪ 🍽 200.
★★ *Royal Montmartre*, 68, bd de Clichy,
☎ (1) 46.06.22.91, 48 rm, 165. Rest. ♦ *Le Chat Noir* Brasserie, 70-80.

Restaurants :
● ♦♦♦♦ *Beauvilliers*, 52, rue Lamarck,
☎ (1) 42.54.54.42, Euro Visa ℗ ♪ 🍽 closed Mon noon and
Sun, 30 Aug-15 Sep. The most blooming decor in Paris
(terraces for fine days). Édouard Carlier, a most capable
restaurateur (like the figure for whom his house is named)
invites you to celebrate the joys of contemporary cuisine :
*filets de rougets en fine escabêche, saumon sauvage au
curry et julienne d'endives, cassolette de petits gris aux
mousserons*. Édouard loves good sherries, so will you.
His cellar holds great Châteaux and the best Burgundies, 300.
● ♦♦ *Clodenis*, 57, rue Caulaincourt, ☎ (1) 46.06.20.26,
AE DC Euro Visa, closed Mon and Sun. Up on the 'butte'
of Montmartre, a young, competent team serves light,
inventive dishes in a rosy dining-room. Game in season, 210-300.
● ♦♦ *Les Chants du Piano (Michel Derbanne)*, 10, rue
Lambert, ☎ 42.62.02.14. Michel Derbane is back on his
feet, playing the 'piano' (a.k.a. the stove) in his usual
inspired style : *sorbet de foie gras, médaillon de lapin,
cocotte de poulet de Bresse truffé, croustillant de chocolat*, 130-210.
● ♦♦ *Les Fusains*, 44, rue Joseph-de-Maistre,
☎ (1) 42.28.03.69, Visa ⚘ ♿ closed Mon and Sun , lunch
and Sep. In a warm, friendly atmosphere, dine at the foot
of Montmartre, on the terrace in summer. Bernard Mathys
serves a fixed-price menu with delights like : *cuisses de
grenouilles au vin d'Alsace, pigeonneau aux trois choux*,
230-350.
● ♦♦ *Les Semailles*, 3, rue Steinlen, ☎ (1) 46.06.37.05,
AE DC Visa ♪ ♿ closed Mon and Sun, 1-15 Feb, 1-31 Jul.
The talented Jean-Jacques Jouteux has moved again.
Telephone in advance to be sure that he is here ; his presence guarantees an excellent meal, 350-400.
● ♦♦ *Poulbot Gourmet*, 39, rue Lamarck, Visa ♪ His
many regulars are enthusiastic about J.-P. Langevin's
tasty specialties : *étuvée d'escargots, marmite de poissons*, 180-200.
● ♦♦ *Moucharabieh*, 4, rue Aimé-Lavy,
☎ (1) 42.64.48.70, AE Visa ⚘ ♪ closed Mon and Sat noon.
The annex of *Wally le Saharien*, serving the famous desert
couscous and new *tajines* : fish, gambas, lobster, spiny
lobster, 150-220.
● ♦♦ *Grandgousier*, 17, av. Rachel, ☎ (1) 43.87.66.12
℗ ♿ closed Sat and Sun , 1 wk in Aug. Excellent food in
a delightful little setting : *salade d'écrevisses et foie gras,
magret de canard au miel de lavande*, 110-220.
♦ *Le Bateau Lavoir*, 8, rue Garreau, ☎ (1) 46.06.02.00 ⚘
♿ closed Jun. Decent food at decent prices, 65-100.

PARIS XIX

✉ 75019

Hotel :
★★ *Parc*, 1, pl. Armand-Carrel, ☎ (1) 42.08.08.37, 51 rm
♨ 250.

Restaurants :
● ♦♦♦ *Le Pavillon Puebla*, Parc des Buttes-Chaumont,
☎ (1) 42.08.92.62, Visa ℗ ♨ ⚘ ♪ closed Sat noon and
Sun. The Vergès family has changed address. Quiet, greenery, luxury and a new decor for this Belle-Époque house.
Original culinary creations : *bouillabaisse glacée, matelote
de filets de sardines à la moelle, sole et langoustines aux
champignons sylvestres*. Tasty wines, 200-250.

● ♦♦ *La Pièce de Boeuf*, 7, rue Corentin Cariou,
☎ 40.05.95.95, closed Sat and Sun. Guy Cardon's cook-

ing is an excellent reason to head up to La Villette. Fine meat specialties washed down with appealing little house wines, 200.

♦♦ *Au Cochon d'Or*, 192, av. Jean-Jaurès, ☎ (1) 46.07.23.13, AE DC Euro Visa. A new setting for grilled beef *spéciale Cochon d'Or, salade de tête de veau*, 200-360.

♦♦ *La Chaumière*, 46, av. Secrétan, ☎ (1) 46.07.98.62, AE DC Euro Visa Ⓟ closed Sun , Aug. Spec : *tartare de langue de veau, lotte au coulis de langoustines*, game in season, 70-160.

PARIS XX

⊠ 75020

Hotels :
★★ *Pyrénées-Gambetta*, 12, av. du Père-Lachaise, ☎ (1) 47.97.76.57, 30 rm ⚲ 265.
★★ *Unic Hôtel*, 6, rue du Pont-de-l'Eure, ☎ (1) 43.61.93.10, 35 rm Ⓟ ⚲ closed Aug, 200.

Restaurants :
♦♦ *Relais des Pyrénées*, 1, rue du Jourdain, ☎ (1) 46.36.65.81, AE DC Euro Visa, closed Sat and Aug. Spec : *confit d'oie comme en Béarn, saumon frais au champagne*, 220-310.
● ♦ *Aux Becs Fins*, 44, bd de Menilmontant, ☎ (1) 47.97.51.52, Visa ♪ The local crowd and those in the know adore Laurence Lefebvre's generous bistro cooking : *foie gras frais, cassoulet du Périgord, Saint-Jacques Laurençais*, 120-240.

Practical holiday guide

Getting to France

air travel   Every major airline flies to France, either to Paris or to another of the country's international airports.
Air France offers the widest range of travel and holiday opportunities, and reservations offices are good information centres for travelers.
The major Parisian airports are **Roissy-Charles de Gaulle** and **Orly.** From Roissy, **Air France shuttle buses** leave every 15 min for Porte Maillot, not far from the Champs-Élysées. **Roissy-Rail** provides trains every 15 min to the Gare du Nord railroad station, then on to the Châtelet metro station.
From Orly, there are **shuttle buses** to Invalides Aérogare terminal in central Paris, with a stop possible at Montparnasse upon request. **Orly-Rail** has trains every 15 min to the Austerlitz, St-Michel and Gare d'Orsay stations.
There is a **helicopter shuttle service** between Roissy and Orly, and also from these airports to a heliport at the Porte de Sèvres (metro : Place Balard) on the S edge of the city. Private air services are available at the **Zone d'Aviation d'Affaires** at Le Bourget Airport, N of Paris, before Roissy.

Air France offices abroad
● **U.K. :** 158 New Bond St., London WIYOA, ☎ (01) 499 8611 ; Heathrow Airport, ☎ (01) 759 2311.
● **U.S.A. : New York :** 666 Fifth Ave., 10019, ☎ (212) 247 0100 ; 1350 Ave. of the Americas, ☎ (212) 841 7300 ; 888 Seventh Ave., ☎ (212) 247 0100 ; Kennedy Airport, ☎ (212) 632 7200. **Chicago and the Midwest :** John Hancock Center, 875 N. Michigan Ave., ☎ (800) 237 2747 ; 22 S. Michigan Ave., ☎ (312) 984 0200 ; O'Hare International Airport, ☎ (312) 686 4531. **Los Angeles :** 510 W. 6th St., ☎ (213) 688 9200 ; 8501 Wilshire Bd., Beverly Hills, ☎ (213) 625 7171 ; L.A. Airport, ☎ (213) 646 0028.
● **Canada : Montréal :** 979 Ouest Bd de Maisonneuve, H3A 1M4, ☎ (514) 285 5060 ; Mirabel Airport, ☎ (514) 476 3838. **Ottawa :** 220 av. Laurier, suite 340, ☎ (613) 236 0689. **Québec :** 2, place Québec, suite 742, ☎ (418) 529 0663. **Toronto :** 151 Bloor St. West, suite 600, ☎ (416) 922 3344. **Vancouver :** 1537 W. Eighth Ave., suite 104, ☎ (604) 733 4151.

information in France
Roissy-Charles de Gaulle, ☎ (1) 48.62.22.80 ; Orly sud/Orly ouest, ☎ (1) 48.84.32.10 ; Air France, ☎ (1) 46.75.78.00 ; Air Inter, ☎ (1) 46.75.12.12 ; Air France offi-

ces : 119, av. des Champs-Élysées, 75008 Paris, plus numerous offices in other French cities; Helicopter shuttle : Hélifrance, Héliport de Paris, ☎ (1) 45.54.95.11/45.57.53.67.

rail

France is linked into Europe's extensive rail system and can be reached from such faraway destinations as Istanbul and even Vladivostock.

ferries

There is continuous service between England and France across the Channel. Only in July and August are last-minute reservations difficult to obtain. Crossings last approx 35 min by hovercraft, and 90 min by traditional ferry. Overnight crossings with cabins are also available.

information

Most travel agents can supply information and reservations, or these can be obtained directly from the ferry companies :
● **Brittany Ferries,** Plymouth, ☎ (07) 52221331.
● **Hoverspeed,** Dover, ☎ (03) 042402 02.
● **Sally-The Viking Line,** Ramsgate, ☎ (08) 43595566.
● **Sealink,** 179 Piccadilly, London W1V OBA, ☎ (01) 3871234.
● **P.O.,** London, 127 Regents St., ☎ (01) 7344431 ; Portsmouth, ☎ (07) 05755521 ; Dover, ☎ (03) 042236 05.

Customs, passports and visas

customs

Visitors to France may import limited amounts of perfume, alcohol and tobacco duty-free. Details of allowances are available at airports, rail and ferry terminals. Allowances are more generous for Common Market members. Foreign currency is not subject to restrictions on entry, but if more than 5 000 French francs are to be re-exported, a "Declaration of Entry" form must be completed and submitted when leaving France.

information

● **French Customs Information Centre,** 182, rue Saint-Honoré, 75001 Paris, ☎ (1) 42.60.35.90.

passports and visas

Visas are NOT required for EEC member countries. However, a valid passport is required to be in your possession when you depart for France.
For stays of 3 months or more, a resident's permit *(carte de séjour)* is mandatory. Apply to nearest French consulate or local *préfecture de police* when in France. EEC members must have a resident's permit in order to work in France. Citizens of other countries must have a work permit which is very difficult to obtain at present. Apply to : 93, av. Armentiers, 75011 Paris.

For U.S. and Canadian citizens, a visa IS required. This must be obtained in a French consulate in your country ·of origin before making airline reservations to France; it cannot be obtained in France. You don't have to wait and there is a slight fee. You can also do it by mail. Brochures concerning work permits for American citizens are available at the American Embassy, 2, rue Saint-Florentin, 75042 Paris Cedex 01, ☎ (1) 42.61.80.75/42.96.14.88. Canadian citizens, contact : Canadian Embassy, 35, av. Montaigne, 75008 Paris, ☎ (1) 47.23.01.01.

Tourist Information

F.G.T.O. The **French Government Tourist Office** is situated in major cities abroad and is, without a doubt, the best source of information for holidays in France. Although the F.G.T.O. does not book travel or accommodation, the staff go out of their way to provide all help necessary for planning holiday arrangements. The F.G.T.O. provides lists of tour operators and travel agents specializing in every holiday field ; for example, travel for the disabled, inland waterways, country and farmhouse holidays, châteaux-hôtels, etc.

The **A.N.I.T.** *(Agence Nationale pour l'Information Touristique)* will provide additional help, while the **C.D.T.s** *(Comités Départementaux du Tourisme)* have complementary information for regions and departments of France. **Loisirs-Accueil** lists complete lodgings.

information
- **A.N.I.T.,** 8, av. de l'Opéra, 75001 Paris, ☎ (1) 42.60.37.38.
- **Air France** and **U.T.A.** offices throughout the world.
- **Direction du Tourisme** (for complaints), 2, rue Linois, 75015 Paris, ☎ (1) 45.75.62.16.
French Tourist Offices abroad :
- **Canada :** 1981 av. McGill College, Tour Esso, Street 490, Montreal QCMH3A2 W9, ☎ (514) 288 4264. 1 Dundas St. W., suite 2405, Box 8, Toronto ONTM5G123, ☎ (416) 593 4717.
- **U.K. :** 178 Piccadilly, London W1V OAL, ☎ (01) 629 12 72.
- **U.S.A. :** 610 Fifth Ave., New York, NY 10020-2452, ☎ (212) 757 1125. 645 N. Michigan Ave., suite 630, Chicago, IL 60611-2836, ☎ (312) 757 7800. World Trade Center, N103 2050 Sternmons Freeway, P.O. Box 58610, Dallas, TX 75258, ☎ (214) 742 7011. 9401 Wilshire Blvd., Beverly Hills, CA 90212, ☎ (213) 271 6665. 1 Hallidie Plaza, suite 250, San Francisco, CA 94102-2818, ☎ (415) 986 4161.

Money

The French monetary unit is the **franc**, which subdivides into 100 centimes. The French use both the term "old" franc and "new" franc which can create confusion; however, prices are always quoted in "new" francs.

All major travelers checks are accepted at French banks. Some hotels, restaurants and shops also accept them, but the exchange rate is less favourable than at a bank.

travelers checks

Visa, which is paired with *Carte Bleue* in France, is the most widely accepted. Some, but not all, hotels, restaurants and shops accept American Express, Diners Club or Eurocard.

credit cards

● In case of loss :
Visa, ☎ (1) 42.77.11.90; American Express, ☎ (1) 47.08.31.21; Diners Club, ☎ (1) 47.62.75.75; Eurocard/Master Charge, ☎ (1) 43.23.46.46.

Emergencies

● Anywhere in France : **Police**, ☎ 17; **Firemen**, ☎ 18.
● In Paris : **ambulances** *(SAMU)*, ☎(1) 45.67.00.00; **poisoning**, ☎ (1) 42.05.63.29; **burns**, St-Antoine Hospital, ☎ (1) 43.33.33.33, *poste* (extension) 23.60; **medical assistance** 24 hrs/day (fee charged), *S.O.S. Médecins*, ☎ (1) 43.37.77.77; **dental emergencies** after 8 pm and Sun., hols., *S.O.S. Dentistes*, ☎ (1) 43.37.51.00.

Post and telephone

Postal and telephone services in France are run by a state-controlled organization, *Poste et Télécommunications* (or *P.T.T.*). Most post offices are open 8 am-7 pm weekdays and 8-12 Saturday. The main post office in Paris, open 24 hrs/day, is located at 52, rue du Louvre, 75001. Telephone directories from the world over can be consulted here.

Direct dialing is possible to anywhere in U.K. and U.S. Pavement (sidewalk) phone booths increasingly accept only a special credit card which may be purchased in a post office (where you may also phone). Be warned that hotels and restaurants charge higher rates for calls made by clients.
Reduced rates exist : −30 % for calls in Europe after 6:30 pm and −70 % after 11 pm, and all day Sunday and national hols. Reduced rates to the U.S. : 10 pm-10 am (French time) and all day Sunday.

telephone

Telephone numbers in France con-

dialing

tain 8 figures. When quoting a number, do it by 10s, e.g. : 42.64.22.22 is "quarante-deux, soixante-quatre, vingt-deux, vingt-deux".

When calling from Paris to the provinces, dial 16 before the 8-figure number.

When calling Paris from the provinces, dial 16.1 before the number.

When calling from province to province, simply dial the 8-figure number.

If in doubt, dial 12 for Information.

Museums and Monuments

France's cultural and artistic heritage is extraordinarily rich. Literally thousands of sites and monuments exist within her borders.

For information concerning all the "châteaux" and classified sites open to the public, as well as cultural voyages, contact :

● **Caisse Nationale des Monuments Historiques et Sites,** Hôtel de Sully, 62, rue Saint-Antoine, 75004 Paris, ☎ (1) 42.74.22.22.

general information

● **Direction des Musées de France,** Palais du Louvre, 75001 Paris, ☎ (1) 42.60.39.26.

For up-to-date information, purchase at newspaper stands *Pariscope, Officiel des Spectacles, Officiel des Galeries,* and *Art Info*.

hints

State museums are closed on Tue., and municipal museums are closed on Mon. Opening hours are extremely variable. An entrance fee is charged.

technological and industrial museums

Information on sites of technical interest may be obtained from local and regional tourist offices and are described in the regional description section of this guide. Factory visits require a written demand ahead of time and are available only to recognized groups. It is possible to visit a dam, solar station or a nuclear power station with guided visits, provided this permission is granted.

archaeology, ecomuseums

This most recent form of archaeology concerns the study and conservation of 19th and early 20thC industrial society. This discipline has produced several ecomuseums. For example, the museum at Le Creusot (Burgundy) relates the story of crystal manufacturing and the founding of the Schneider mining empire. In N France, ecomuseums preserve the history of the textile industry in Fourmies, glass manufacturing in Sars, woodwork in Felleries, and mining in Lewarde (near Douai).

technical tourism

Mulhouse has become the leader in this form of tourism, and among the museums to be visited are : the "Musée National de l'Automobile", the Railway Museum, the Electrical Museum, and the Printed-Fabrics Museum.

Index